Now glory be to God, who by his mighty power at work within us is able to do far more than we would ever dare to ask or even dream of—infinitely beyond our highest prayers, desires, thoughts, or hopes.

EPHESIANS 3:20 TLB

40 Days
small groups
Start 9/12/18

* I stepped away to
not Lead = asking Debbie –
Diane – Christine + Renee to
lead..
Trusting God to help me and to
release all pressures + fears..
Help me Jesus to trust you!

40 Days to a Powerful Prayer Life

WARREN

Contents

Resources

Understanding Your Study Guide

Here is a brief explanation of the features of this study guide.

WEEKEND SERMON NOTES

Bring this book to church during your 40 Days of Prayer campaign. Use these pages to take notes on your pastor's weekly sermons.

CHECKING IN

Begin each group conversation by briefly discussing a question that will help focus everyone's attention on the subject of the lesson.

KEY VERSE

Each week you will find a key Bible verse for your group to focus on together. If someone in the group has a different translation, ask them to read it out loud so the group can get a bigger picture of the meaning of the passage.

VIDEO LESSON

There is a video lesson for the group to watch together each week. Fill in the blanks in the lesson outline as you watch the video, and be sure to refer back to these outline during your discussion time.

DISCOVERY QUESTIONS

Discuss these questions as a group. Choose the questions that seem right for the group. The point is to learn and grow together in your faith as you discuss the session, even if this means you don't get to all of the questions.

PUTTING IT INTO PRACTICE

We don't just want to be hearers of the Word, we also need to be doers of the Word (James 1:22). This section contains suggestions for your group and for you individually to apply the things you are learning.

DAILY PRAYER JOURNAL

This section contains directions for daily devotions, including Bible verses and Daily Prayer Journal prompts.

There are additional small group resources such as SMALL GROUP GUIDELINES, HELPS FOR HOSTS, SMALL GROUP CALENDAR, etc., in the back of this guide.

A TIP FOR THE HOST

The study guide material is meant to be your servant, not your master. The point is not to race through the sessions—the point is to take time to let God work in your lives. Give your group members time to explore the questions and process what they learned in each session. It is not necessary to "go around the circle" before you move on to the next question. Let your group know they have the freedom to speak up and share, but don't insist on it. Your group will enjoy deeper, more open sharing and discussion if there is an atmosphere of acceptance and they don't feel pressured to speak up.

How to Use This Video Curriculum

Follow these simple steps for a successful small group meeting:

- Open your group meeting by using the CHECKING IN section of your study guide.

- WATCH THE VIDEO lesson together and follow along in the outlines in this study guide.

- Complete the rest of the discussion materials for each session, including the OUTLINE and DISCOVERY QUESTIONS. Be sure to review the PUTTING IT INTO PRACTICE section that helps you implement the lessons into your daily life. Commit to filling out the DAILY PRAYER JOURNAL section each day.

- Close your time together by praying as a group and planning your next session.

Week
One

Weekend
Sermon Notes

_____

_____

_____

_____

_____

_____

_____

_____

_____

_____

_____

_____

_____

_____

_____

_____

_____

THE PURPOSE OF PRAYER

CHECKING IN

Before you begin this study, review the Small Group Guidelines
on page 202 of this study guide.

What does prayer mean to you?

KEY VERSE

*"If you remain in me and my words remain in you,
ask whatever you wish, and it will be given you."*
JOHN 15:7 (NIV)

Watch the video lesson now and follow along in your outline.

THE PURPOSE OF PRAYER

Prayer is God's idea. If he didn't want to hear from you, he wouldn't invite you to pray. God wants to hear from you because he loves you. He cares about every detail of your life. There is nothing too big or too small for his attention.

FOUR PRIMARY PURPOSES FOR PRAYER

- **Prayer is an act of** _____ .

"I am the vine; you are the branches. If you remain in me and I in you, you will bear much fruit; apart from me you can do nothing. If you do not remain in me, you are like a branch that is thrown away and withers; such branches are picked up, thrown into the fire and burned. If you remain in me and my words remain in you, ask whatever you wish, and it will be given you."
JOHN 15:5–7 (NIV)

- **Prayer is an act of** _____ .

"I no longer call you servants, because a servant does not know his master's business. Instead, I have called you friends, for everything that I learned from my Father I have made known to you. You did not choose me, but I chose you and appointed you to go and bear fruit—fruit that will last. Then the Father will give you whatever you ask in my name."
JOHN 15:15–16 (NIV)

- **Prayer is an act of** _____ .

Do not be anxious about anything, but in everything by prayer and supplication with thanksgiving let your requests be made known to God. And the peace of God, which surpasses all understanding, will guard your hearts and your minds in Christ Jesus.
PHILIPPIANS 4:6–7 (ESV)

"I tell you the truth, my Father will give you whatever you ask in my name. Until now you have not asked for anything in my name. Ask and you will receive, and your joy will be complete."
JOHN 16:23–24 (NIV)

You don't have what you want because you don't ask God for it.
JAMES 4:2 (NLT)

He fulfills the desires of those who reverence and trust him.
PSALM 145:19 (TLB)

Delight yourself in the Lord and he will give you the desires of your heart.
PSALM 37:4 (NIV)

"Which of you, if his son asks for bread, will give him a stone? Or if he asks for a fish, will give him a snake? If you, then, though you are evil, know how to give good gifts to your children, how much more will your Father in heaven give good gifts to those who ask him!"
MATTHEW 7:9–11 (NIV)

- **Prayer is an act of** _____ .

Prayer is God's way of letting us partner with him to accomplish his purposes.

"I tell you the truth, anyone who has faith in me will do what I have been doing. He will do even greater things than these because I am going to the Father."
JOHN 14:12 (NIV)

"And I will do whatever you ask in my name, so that the Son may bring glory to the Father. You may ask me for anything in my name, and I will do it."
JOHN 14:13–14 (NIV)

Your prayers release the power of God into the most hopeless situations. They can penetrate places where no man or woman can go, whether that's a closed, international border, or the hardened heart of a skeptic. Prayer makes the impossible possible.

The king's heart is in the hand of the Lord; he directs it like a watercourse wherever he pleases.
PROVERBS 21:1 (NIV)

Discovery Questions

Please don't feel pressured to discuss every discovery question. It's okay to choose the questions that are right for your group. The point is not to race through the session; the point is to take time to let God work in your lives.

- **What role has prayer played in shaping your relationship with God?**

_____

_____

_____

- **Based on today's lesson about the purpose of prayer, what can you do to deepen your conversation with God?**

_____

_____

_____

- **What are you hoping to get out of this study in the next forty days?**

_____

_____

_____

Praying together is one of the great privileges of small group life.

Putting It Into Practice

We don't just want to be hearers of the Word, we also need to be doers of the Word (James 1:22). This section contains suggestions for your group and for you individually to apply the things you are learning. Be sure to leave time each week to review this material.

If praying in a group is new or uncomfortable for you, we encourage you to start by praying single-sentence prayers. Don't worry about how fancy you sound. God isn't looking for eloquence. He just wants honesty. Talk to God like you talk to a friend. Give everyone a chance to pray, but don't insist on it. Over time, your group will feel much more comfortable praying together. Pray for one another and for your church family as you begin 40 Days of Prayer.

IN YOUR GROUP
PRAY TOGETHER

What are you lacking in your life simply because you've never asked God for it? What is your greatest need? Don't hold back. Share your prayer request with your group, then pray together. You can record your prayer requests in Our Prayers & Praise on page 204 of this study guide.

NOTES:

IN YOUR LIFE
DAILY PRAYER

Set a daily alarm as a reminder to pause and pray this week. This idea works best if you pick the same time every day. Are you a morning person? Then pick a time in the morning. If you're more alert in the afternoon or evening, then choose a time that fits the way you're wired. The best time to pray is when you're at your best. Consistency is more important that quantity; it's more important to be mindful to pray every day this week than it is to spend a lengthy time in prayer on one or two days. If you're already consistent with your prayer time, or you're looking for a way to get started with prayer, then turn to the Daily Prayer of Surrender on page 176.

NOTES:

_____

_____

_____

_____

_____

_____

_____

Daily Prayer Journal

Starting on page 22 you will find Bible verses and daily prayer journal prompts for The Purpose of Prayer. Take a few minutes each day to read the verse several times, slowly. Emphasize a different word or phrase each time you read the passage. Underline key words or phrases that are especially meaningful to you. Follow the prompts and write down your responses in the journal space provided. Finish with a prayer.

Before You Go

WHAT DECISIONS DO YOU NEED TO MAKE AS A GROUP THIS WEEK?

Healthy groups share responsibilities and group ownership. Turn to the Small Group Calendar on page 206 of this study guide. Fill out the calendar together, at least for next week, noting where you will meet each week, who will facilitate your meeting, and who will provide a meal or snack. Note special events, socials, or days off as well. Your Group Host will be very appreciative, and everyone will have a lot more fun together. Coordinating the group calendar is a great role for someone in your group to fill. Also start collecting basic contact information, including phone numbers and email addresses. The Small Group Roster on page 207 of your study guide is a good place to record this information.

Daily
Prayer
Journal

"I am the vine; you are the branches. If you remain in me and I in you, you will bear much fruit; apart from me you can do nothing. If you do not remain in me, you are like a branch that is thrown away and withers; such branches are picked up, thrown into the fire and burned. If you remain in me and my words remain in you, ask whatever you wish, and it will be given you."

JOHN 15:5–7 (NIV)

Day 1

What did you hear?

What did God say to you as you read today's Bible passage?
What word or phrase was most meaningful to you?

_____

_____

_____

_____

What do you think?

What does this passage mean to you? How does it apply to your life?

_____

_____

_____

_____

What is your prayer?

This is where you turn your thoughts into prayer. It could be a prayer of gratitude or
praise. It could be a prayer of confession or a request for God's help. It's up to you.
But take a minute to write a prayer of response to God.

_____

_____

_____

"I no longer call you servants, because a servant does not know his master's business. Instead, I have called you friends, for everything that I learned from my Father I have made known to you. You did not choose me, but I chose you and appointed you to go and bear fruit— fruit that will last. Then the Father will give you whatever you ask in my name."

JOHN 15:15–16 (NIV)

Day 2   9/11/18

What did you hear?

What did God say to you as you read today's Bible passage?
What word or phrase was most meaningful to you?

God chose me = I did it chose Him
He has chosen me to bear fruit =
Fruit that will last.

What do you think?

What does this passage mean to you? How does it apply to your life?

Having all the duties of alison / baby /
(Heartbreak) Upcoming Retreat -
Sept 21-23 = feeling so overwhelmed
by pressure = God is saying = I have
chosen you to bear fruit.

What is your prayer?

This is where you turn your thoughts into prayer. It could be a prayer of gratitude or praise. It could be a prayer of confession or a request for God's help. It's up to you. But take a minute to write a prayer of response to God.

Lord - I'm overwhelmed - sad and lonely
in my pain and feel isolated.
Please help me to trust you for the
strength + fruit to do what you
have placed on me. Thank you!

Do not be anxious about anything, but in everything by prayer and supplication with thanksgiving let your requests be made known to God. And the peace of God, which surpasses all understanding, will guard your hearts and your minds in Christ Jesus.

PHILIPPIANS 4:6–7 (ESV)

Day 3

What did you hear?

What did God say to you as you read today's Bible passage?
What word or phrase was most meaningful to you?

_____

_____

_____

_____

What do you think?

What does this passage mean to you? How does it apply to your life?

_____

_____

_____

_____

What is your prayer?

This is where you turn your thoughts into prayer. It could be a prayer of gratitude or
praise. It could be a prayer of confession or a request for God's help. It's up to you.
But take a minute to write a prayer of response to God.

_____

_____

_____

_____

"*I tell you the truth, my Father will give you whatever you ask in my name. Until now you have not asked for anything in my name. Ask and you will receive, and your joy will be complete.*"

JOHN 16:23–24 (NIV)

Day 4

What did you hear?

What did God say to you as you read today's Bible passage?
What word or phrase was most meaningful to you?

_____

_____

_____

_____

What do you think?

What does this passage mean to you? How does it apply to your life?

_____

_____

_____

_____

What is your prayer?

This is where you turn your thoughts into prayer. It could be a prayer of gratitude or
praise. It could be a prayer of confession or a request for God's help. It's up to you.
But take a minute to write a prayer of response to God.

_____

_____

_____

Delight yourself in the Lord and he will give you the desires of your heart.

PSALM 37:4 (NIV)

Day 5

What did you hear?

What did God say to you as you read today's Bible passage?
What word or phrase was most meaningful to you?

_____

_____

_____

_____

What do you think?

What does this passage mean to you? How does it apply to your life?

_____

_____

_____

_____

What is your prayer?

This is where you turn your thoughts into prayer. It could be a prayer of gratitude or
praise. It could be a prayer of confession or a request for God's help. It's up to you.
But take a minute to write a prayer of response to God.

_____

_____

_____

"I tell you the truth, anyone who has faith in me will do what I have been doing. He will do even greater things than these because I am going to the Father."

JOHN 14:12 (NIV)

Day 6

What did you hear?

What did God say to you as you read today's Bible passage?
What word or phrase was most meaningful to you?

_____

_____

_____

_____

What do you think?

What does this passage mean to you? How does it apply to your life?

_____

_____

_____

_____

What is your prayer?

This is where you turn your thoughts into prayer. It could be a prayer of gratitude or
praise. It could be a prayer of confession or a request for God's help. It's up to you.
But take a minute to write a prayer of response to God.

_____

_____

_____

"And I will do whatever you ask in my name, so that the Son may bring glory to the Father. You may ask me for anything in my name, and I will do it."

JOHN 14:13–14 (NIV)

Day 7

What did you hear?

What did God say to you as you read today's Bible passage?
What word or phrase was most meaningful to you?

_____

_____

_____

_____

What do you think?

What does this passage mean to you? How does it apply to your life?

_____

_____

_____

_____

What is your prayer?

This is where you turn your thoughts into prayer. It could be a prayer of gratitude or
praise. It could be a prayer of confession or a request for God's help. It's up to you.
But take a minute to write a prayer of response to God.

_____

_____

_____

Week
Two

Weekend Sermon Notes

_____

_____

_____

_____

_____

_____

_____

_____

_____

_____

_____

_____

_____

_____

_____

_____

_____

HOW TO PRAY WITH CONFIDENCE

CHECKING IN

Was there an insight from your Daily Prayer Journal that was especially meaningful to you this week?

KEY VERSE

Cast all your care upon him, for he cares for you.
1 PETER 5:7 (NKJV)

Watch the video lesson now and follow along in your outline.

HOW TO PRAY WITH CONFIDENCE

Jesus taught us to pray, "Our Father in heaven." One of the words in the Bible for "father" is "Abba," which simply means "daddy" or "papa." Abba is a term of endearment, love, intimacy, and security. Jesus was telling us that when you pray to God, you're talking to your Dad.

When you truly know and understand your heavenly Father, it will radically change your prayer life. It will enable you to pray with more confidence than ever before.

- God is a _____Caring_____ Father.

"Can a mother forget the baby at her breast and have no compassion on the child she has borne? Though she may forget, I will not forget you!"
ISAIAH 49:15 (NIV)

For I am convinced that neither death nor life, neither angels nor demons, neither the present nor the future, nor any powers, neither height nor depth, nor anything else in all creation, will be able to separate us from the love of God that is in Christ Jesus our Lord.
ROMANS 8:38–39 (NIV)

Cast all your care upon him, for he cares for you.
1 PETER 5:7 (NKJV)

• God is a _Consistent_ Father.

There is nothing deceitful in God, nothing two-faced, nothing fickle.
JAMES 1:17 (THE MESSAGE)

"I the Lord do not change."
MALACHI 3:6 (NIV)

Even when we are too weak to have any faith left, [God] remains faithful to us and will help us, for he cannot disown us who are a part of himself, and he will always carry out his promises to us.
2 TIMOTHY 2:13 (TLB)

[God] will never go back on his promises.
ROMANS 11:29 (TLB)

My God is changeless in his love for me.
PSALM 59:10 (TLB)

• God is a _Close_ Father.

"I will not in any way fail you nor give you up nor leave you without support. I will not, I will not, I will not in any degree leave you helpless nor forsake nor let you down or relax my hold on you. Assuredly not!"
HEBREWS 13:5 (AMP)

How precious are your thoughts about me, O God. They cannot be numbered! I can't even count them; they outnumber the grains of sand!
PSALM 139:17–18 (NLT)

- God is never _To busy For me_.

Though my father and mother forsake me, the Lord will receive me.
PSALM 27:10 (NIV)

- God loves to _Meet my needs_.

"If you, then, though you are evil, know how to give good gifts to your children, how much more will your Father in heaven give good gifts to those who ask him!"
MATTHEW 7:11 (NIV)

- God is _Sympathetic to my hurts_.

The Lord is close to the brokenhearted and saves those who are crushed in spirit.
PSALM 34:18 (NIV)

God is our refuge and strength, an ever-present help in times of trouble.
PSALM 46:1 (GW)

- God is a _Competent_ Father.

"Nothing is impossible for God!"
LUKE 1:37 (CEV)

[God] is able to do far more than we would ever dare to ask or even dream of—infinitely beyond our highest prayers, desires, thoughts, or hopes.
EPHESIANS 3:20 (TLB)

No eye has seen, no ear has heard, and no mind has imagined the things that God has prepared for those who love him.
1 CORINTHIANS 2:9 (GW)

Are you certain that God is your Father?

To all who received him, to those who believed in his name, he gave the right to become children of God.
JOHN 1:12 (NIV)

When you place your faith in Jesus Christ, then God becomes your caring, consistent, close, competent Father, and you can pray with confidence the way Jesus taught us to pray: "*My* Father in heaven, hallowed be your name."

You are all God's children by believing in Christ Jesus.
GALATIANS 3:26 (GW)

Discovery
Questions

Please don't feel pressured to discuss every discovery question. It's okay to choose the questions that are right for your group. The point is not to race through the session; the point is to take time to let God work in your lives.

- **Did anyone pray the Salvation Prayer with Pastor Rick? If so, take time as a group to congratulate and pray for that person.**

_____

_____

_____

_____

- **In this session, we learned that God is a caring, consistent, close, and competent Father. Which of these characteristics has the greatest meaning to you, and why?**

_____

_____

_____

_____

- Read Ephesians 3:20 in the outline above. Pastor Rick says, "Think of your biggest problem, your greatest dream, your most daunting challenge or fear. Not only can God handle it, he can do more than you can even imagine." What are you asking God to do? Is there something you're afraid to ask for or dream of? God can handle it all.

- Psalm 34:18 says, *"The Lord is close to the brokenhearted and saves those who are crushed in spirit"* (NIV). Has this been true for you? If so, share your experience with the group.

Putting It Into Practice

We don't just want to be hearers of the Word, we also need to be doers of the Word (James 1:22). This section contains suggestions for your group and for you individually to apply the things you are learning. Be sure to leave time each week to review this material.

IN YOUR GROUP
PRAY TOGETHER

Take this time to pray with confidence for anyone in your group who may be in a season of heartbreak or experiencing a crushed spirit. You can record your prayer requests in Our Prayers & Praise on page 204 of this study guide. This is also a great time to pray for other people in your lives who may be in the midst of a challenging life circumstance or problem.

NOTES:

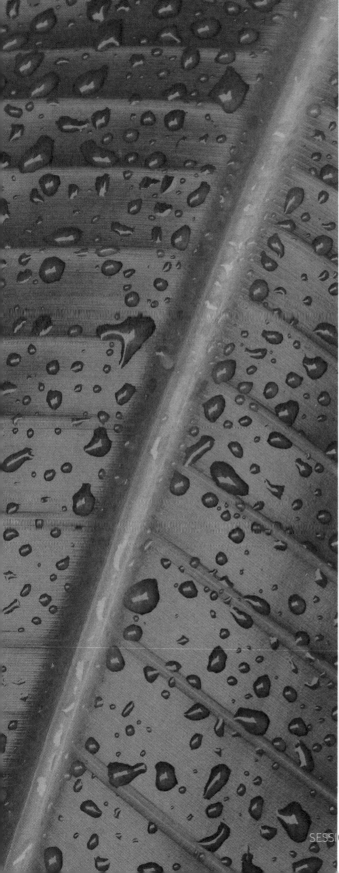

IN YOUR LIFE
PRAY WITH CONFIDENCE

Turn to the Ephesians 3:20 Exercise on page 177. Take a few moments to soak in the truth that God can do more than you can ever ask or imagine. Journal your response to this Scripture. Take your time with this. We will encourage you to share your thoughts with your group as you start the next session.

NOTES:

_____

_____

_____

_____

_____

_____

_____

Daily Prayer Journal

Starting on page 50 you will find Bible verses and daily prayer journal prompts for How to Pray with Confidence. Take a few minutes every day to read each verse several times, slowly. Emphasize a different word or phrase each time you read the passage. Underline key words or phrases that are especially meaningful to you. Follow the prompts and write down your responses in the journal space provided. Finish with a prayer.

Before You Go

Update the Small Group Calendar on page 206 of this study guide, as needed. Where you will meet each week, who will facilitate your meeting, and who will provide a meal or snack? Note any changes to your calendar. Also add contact information in the Small Group Roster on page 207 of your study guide for new members of your group.

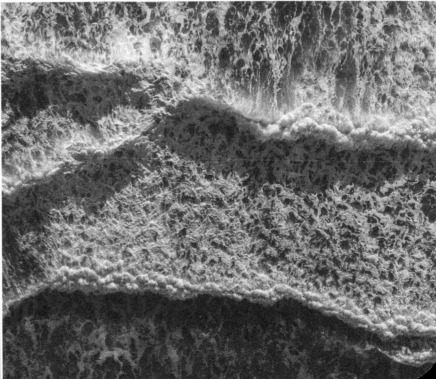

Daily
Prayer
Journal

For I am convinced that neither death nor life, neither angels nor demons, neither the present nor the future, nor any powers, neither height nor depth, nor anything else in all creation, will be able to separate us from the love of God that is in Christ Jesus our Lord.

ROMANS 8:38–39 (NIV)

Day 8

What did you hear?

What did God say to you as you read today's Bible passage?
What word or phrase was most meaningful to you?

_____

_____

_____

_____

What do you think?

What does this passage mean to you? How does it apply to your life?

_____

_____

_____

_____

What is your prayer?

This is where you turn your thoughts into prayer. It could be a prayer of gratitude or praise. It could be a prayer of confession or a request for God's help. It's up to you. But take a minute to write a prayer of response to God.

_____

_____

_____

_____

Even when we are too weak to have any faith left, [God] remains faithful to us and will help us, for he cannot disown us who are a part of himself, and he will always carry out his promises to us.

2 TIMOTHY 2:13 (TLB)

Day 9

What did you hear?

What did God say to you as you read today's Bible passage?
What word or phrase was most meaningful to you?

_____

_____

_____

_____

What do you think?

What does this passage mean to you? How does it apply to your life?

_____

_____

_____

_____

What is your prayer?

This is where you turn your thoughts into prayer. It could be a prayer of gratitude or praise. It could be a prayer of confession or a request for God's help. It's up to you. But take a minute to write a prayer of response to God.

_____

_____

_____

_____

"I will not in any way fail you nor give you up nor leave you without support. I will not, I will not, I will not in any degree leave you helpless nor forsake nor let you down or relax my hold on you. Assuredly not!"

HEBREWS 13:5 (AMP)

Day 10

What did you hear?

What did God say to you as you read today's Bible passage?
What word or phrase was most meaningful to you?

_____

_____

_____

What do you think?

What does this passage mean to you? How does it apply to your life?

_____

_____

_____

_____

What is your prayer?

This is where you turn your thoughts into prayer. It could be a prayer of gratitude or praise. It could be a prayer of confession or a request for God's help. It's up to you. But take a minute to write a prayer of response to God.

_____

_____

_____

_____

How precious are your thoughts about me, O God. They cannot be numbered! I can't even count them; they outnumber the grains of sand!

PSALM 139:17–18 (NLT)

Day 11

What did you hear?

What did God say to you as you read today's Bible passage?
What word or phrase was most meaningful to you?

_____

_____

_____

_____

What do you think?

What does this passage mean to you? How does it apply to your life?

_____

_____

_____

_____

What is your prayer?

This is where you turn your thoughts into prayer. It could be a prayer of gratitude or praise. It could be a prayer of confession or a request for God's help. It's up to you. But take a minute to write a prayer of response to God.

_____

_____

_____

_____

"If you, then, though you are evil, know how to give good gifts to your children, how much more will your Father in heaven give good gifts to those who ask him!"

MATTHEW 7:11 (NIV)

Day 12

What did you hear?

What did God say to you as you read today's Bible passage?
What word or phrase was most meaningful to you?

_____

_____

_____

_____

What do you think?

What does this passage mean to you? How does it apply to your life?

_____

_____

_____

_____

What is your prayer?

This is where you turn your thoughts into prayer. It could be a prayer of gratitude or
praise. It could be a prayer of confession or a request for God's help. It's up to you.
But take a minute to write a prayer of response to God.

_____

_____

_____

_____

*No eye has seen, no ear has heard,
and no mind has imagined the things
that God has prepared for those
who love him.*

1 CORINTHIANS 2:9 (GW)

Day 13

What did you hear?

What did God say to you as you read today's Bible passage?
What word or phrase was most meaningful to you?

_____

_____

_____

_____

What do you think?

What does this passage mean to you? How does it apply to your life?

_____

_____

_____

_____

What is your prayer?

This is where you turn your thoughts into prayer. It could be a prayer of gratitude or praise. It could be a prayer of confession or a request for God's help. It's up to you. But take a minute to write a prayer of response to God.

_____

_____

_____

_____

To all who received him, to those who believed in his name, he gave the right to become children of God.

JOHN 1:12 (NIV)

Day 14

What did you hear?

What did God say to you as you read today's Bible passage?
What word or phrase was most meaningful to you?

_____

_____

_____

_____

What do you think?

What does this passage mean to you? How does it apply to your life?

_____

_____

_____

_____

What is your prayer?

This is where you turn your thoughts into prayer. It could be a prayer of gratitude or praise. It could be a prayer of confession or a request for God's help. It's up to you. But take a minute to write a prayer of response to God.

_____

_____

_____

_____

Week
Three

Weekend
Sermon Notes

_____

_____

_____

_____

_____

_____

_____

_____

_____

_____

_____

_____

_____

_____

_____

_____

THE PATTERN FOR PRAYER (PART ONE)

CHECKING IN

Would anyone like to share their response to the Ephesians 3:20 Exercise or an insight from your Daily Prayer Journal that especially stood out to you this week?

KEY VERSE

Give thanks to the Lord for his unfailing love
and his wonderful deeds for men.
PSALM 107:15 (NIV)

Watch the video lesson now and follow along in your outline.

THE PATTERN FOR PRAYER (PART ONE)

"This, then, is how you should pray."
MATTHEW 6:9 (NIV)

Jesus didn't say, "This is *what* you should pray." He said, "This is *how* you should pray." The Lord's Prayer is not a magic spell or incantation. Instead, the Lord's Prayer is a pattern for prayer.

"Our Father in heaven, hallowed be your name. Your kingdom come. Your will be done on earth as it is in heaven. Give us this day our daily bread. And forgive us our sins, as we forgive those who sin against us. And lead us not into temptation, but deliver us from evil. For yours is the kingdom and the power and the glory forever. Amen."
MATTHEW 6:9–13

The Lord's Prayer is a ten-step pathway that will lead you to a deeper, closer relationship with God.

Step 1: I remember _____.

The Prayer of Connection—*"Our Father in heaven."*

May your roots go down deep into the soil of God's marvelous love; and may you be able to feel and understand, as all God's children should, how long, how wide, how deep, and how high his love really is; and to experience this love for yourselves, though it is so great that you will never see the end of it or fully know or understand it.
EPHESIANS 3:17–19 (TLB)

God's love is long enough to last forever, wide enough to embrace everything about you, deep enough to pull you out of your deepest despair, and high enough to overlook every offense.

Step 2: I tell God _____.

The Prayer of Refocusing—*"Hallowed be your name."*

God's names tell us who he is. He is your Creator who made you, your Father who loves you, and your Savior who forgives you. He is your Shepherd who guides you, and your Shield who hides you. He is your Counselor who gives you wisdom, and your Comforter who gives you strength. He is the best Friend you will ever have.

Give thanks to the Lord for his unfailing love and his wonderful deeds for men.
PSALM 107:15 (NIV)

Step 3: I offer my life _____.

The Prayer of Cooperation—*"Your kingdom come."*

"I know the plans I have for you . . . plans to prosper you and not to harm you, plans to give you hope and a future."
JEREMIAH 29:11 (NIV)

Even when you can't make sense of the troubles you're going through, you can be confident that God is watching out for you and is working everything out for your good.

We know that all that happens to us is working for our good if we love God and are fitting into his plans.
ROMANS 8:28 (TLB)

Living for God's purposes isn't a one-time decision. It has to be a daily attitude of your heart.

So here's what I want you to do, God helping you: Take your everyday, ordinary life—your sleeping, eating, going-to-work, and walking-around life—and place it before God as an offering. Embracing what God does for you is the best thing you can do for him.
ROMANS 12:1 (THE MESSAGE)

Step 4: I give God _____ .

The Prayer of Surrender—*"Your will be done on earth as it is in heaven."*

"Abba, Father," he said, "everything is possible for you. Take this cup from me. Yet not what I will, but what you will."
MARK 14:36 (NIV)

That's the prayer Jesus prayed on his way to the cross. In his hour of deepest suffering, he prayed the Prayer of Surrender. He gave God his pain and sorrow, and he surrendered to the will of God.

Step 5: I trust God _____ .

The Prayer of Dependence—*"Give us this day our daily bread."*

Now that you have told your heavenly Father you love him, and you have surrendered to his will, bring him your prayer requests. He cares about everything that's on your mind. Tell him about the challenges you are facing today, the needs that you have, and the fears and worries that are nagging you.

My God will meet all your needs.
PHILIPPIANS 4:19 (NIV)

Jesus teaches us to ask for daily bread because God wants you to depend on him one day at a time.

"Do not worry about tomorrow, for tomorrow will worry about itself. Each day has enough trouble of its own."
MATTHEW 6:34 (NIV)

Discovery Questions

Choose the questions that are right for your group and take time to let God work in your lives.

- **Prayer starts with who God is; it doesn't start with what you need. Why do you think Jesus taught us to praise God (hallowed be your name) and to surrender to God (your kingdom come, your will be done) before we make our requests to God?**

_____

_____

_____

- **Pastor Rick listed some of the names of God: Creator, Father, Savior, Shepherd, Shield, Counselor, Comforter, and Friend. Which name reminds you most of God's presence in your life or resonates with you in your current circumstance?**

_____

_____

_____

- **The Lord's Prayer teaches us to ask God for our daily bread. Share a story of how God has provided for you.**

_____

_____

_____

Putting It Into Practice

Be doers of the Word by applying the things you are learning.

PRAY TOGETHER

Before you begin praying as a group, share your individual prayer requests based on what stood out to you as an area of growth in this session. Now pray as a group. Remember to start with praise, then surrender your will to God's will, and then make your requests.

GRATITUDE LIST

This week start your daily prayer time with praise and worship. Notice what happens in your prayer life. Turn to the Gratitude List: God's Goodness to Me from A–Z on page 178. Fill out a few things you are grateful for today. You don't need to complete the list; just simply get started. God loves when we come to him with an attitude of gratitude.

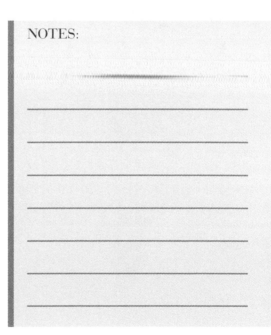

NOTES:

_____

_____

_____

_____

_____

_____

Daily Prayer Journal

Starting on page 76 you will find Bible verses and daily prayer journal prompts for The Pattern for Prayer (Part One). Take a few minutes every day to read each verse several times, slowly. Emphasize a different word or phrase each time you read the passage. Underline key words or phrases that are especially meaningful to you. Follow the prompts and write down your responses in the journal space provided. Finish with a prayer.

NOTES:

Daily
Prayer
Journal

"Our Father in heaven, hallowed be your name. Your kingdom come. Your will be done on earth as it is in heaven. Give us this day our daily bread. And forgive us our sins, as we forgive those who sin against us. And lead us not into temptation, but deliver us from evil. For yours is the kingdom and the power and the glory forever. Amen."

MATTHEW 6:9–13

Day 15

What did you hear?

What did God say to you as you read today's Bible passage?
What word or phrase was most meaningful to you?

_____

_____

_____

_____

What do you think?

What does this passage mean to you? How does it apply to your life?

_____

_____

_____

_____

What is your prayer?

This is where you turn your thoughts into prayer. It could be a prayer of gratitude or praise. It could be a prayer of confession or a request for God's help. It's up to you. But take a minute to write a prayer of response to God.

_____

_____

_____

_____

May your roots go down deep into the soil of God's marvelous love; and may you be able to feel and understand, as all God's children should, how long, how wide, how deep, and how high his love really is; and to experience this love for yourselves, though it is so great that you will never see the end of it or fully know or understand it.

EPHESIANS 3:17–19 (TLB)

Day 16

What did you hear?

What did God say to you as you read today's Bible passage?
What word or phrase was most meaningful to you?

_____

_____

_____

_____

What do you think?

What does this passage mean to you? How does it apply to your life?

_____

_____

_____

_____

What is your prayer?

This is where you turn your thoughts into prayer. It could be a prayer of gratitude or praise. It could be a prayer of confession or a request for God's help. It's up to you. But take a minute to write a prayer of response to God.

_____

_____

_____

_____

Give thanks to the Lord for his unfailing love and his wonderful deeds for men.

PSALM 107:15 (NIV)

Day 17

What did you hear?

What did God say to you as you read today's Bible passage?
What word or phrase was most meaningful to you?

_____

_____

_____

_____

What do you think?

What does this passage mean to you? How does it apply to your life?

_____

_____

_____

_____

What is your prayer?

This is where you turn your thoughts into prayer. It could be a prayer of gratitude or praise. It could be a prayer of confession or a request for God's help. It's up to you. But take a minute to write a prayer of response to God.

_____

_____

_____

_____

We know that all that happens to us is working for our good if we love God and are fitting into his plans.

ROMANS 8:28 (TLB)

Day 18

What did you hear?

What did God say to you as you read today's Bible passage?
What word or phrase was most meaningful to you?

_____

_____

_____

_____

What do you think?

What does this passage mean to you? How does it apply to your life?

_____

_____

_____

_____

What is your prayer?

This is where you turn your thoughts into prayer. It could be a prayer of gratitude or
praise. It could be a prayer of confession or a request for God's help. It's up to you.
But take a minute to write a prayer of response to God.

_____

_____

_____

_____

So here's what I want you to do,
God helping you: Take your
everyday, ordinary life—your
sleeping, eating, going-to-work,
and walking-around life—and place it
before God as an offering. Embracing
what God does for you is the best
thing you can do for him.

ROMANS 12:1 (THE MESSAGE)

Day 19

What did you hear?

What did God say to you as you read today's Bible passage?
What word or phrase was most meaningful to you?

_____

_____

_____

_____

What do you think?

What does this passage mean to you? How does it apply to your life?

_____

_____

_____

_____

What is your prayer?

This is where you turn your thoughts into prayer. It could be a prayer of gratitude or praise. It could be a prayer of confession or a request for God's help. It's up to you. But take a minute to write a prayer of response to God.

_____

_____

_____

_____

"Abba, Father," he said,
"everything is possible for you.
Take this cup from me. Yet not what
I will, but what you will."

MARK 14:36 (NIV)

Day 20

What did you hear?

What did God say to you as you read today's Bible passage?
What word or phrase was most meaningful to you?

_____

_____

_____

_____

What do you think?

What does this passage mean to you? How does it apply to your life?

_____

_____

_____

_____

What is your prayer?

This is where you turn your thoughts into prayer. It could be a prayer of gratitude or
praise. It could be a prayer of confession or a request for God's help. It's up to you.
But take a minute to write a prayer of response to God.

_____

_____

_____

_____

"Do not worry about tomorrow,
for tomorrow will worry about itself.
Each day has enough trouble
of its own."

MATTHEW 6:34 (NIV)

Day 21

What did you hear?

What did God say to you as you read today's Bible passage?
What word or phrase was most meaningful to you?

_____

_____

_____

_____

What do you think?

What does this passage mean to you? How does it apply to your life?

_____

_____

_____

_____

What is your prayer?

This is where you turn your thoughts into prayer. It could be a prayer of gratitude or
praise. It could be a prayer of confession or a request for God's help. It's up to you.
But take a minute to write a prayer of response to God.

_____

_____

_____

_____

Week
Four

Weekend
Sermon Notes

_____

_____

_____

_____

_____

_____

_____

_____

_____

_____

_____

_____

_____

_____

_____

_____

_____

THE PATTERN FOR PRAYER (PART TWO)

CHECKING IN

Does anyone want to share one or two items from your Gratitude List?

KEY VERSE

Not to us, O Lord, not to us but to your name be the glory;
because of your love and faithfulness.
PSALM 115:1 (NIV)

Watch the video lesson now and follow along in your outline.

THE PATTERN FOR PRAYER (PART TWO)

Step 6: I admit _____ .

The Prayer of Cleansing—*"Forgive us our sins."*

God promises that if you will confess your sins to him, he will forgive you instantly, freely, completely, and permanently.

If we confess our sins to God, he can always be trusted to forgive us and take our sins away.
1 JOHN 1:9 (CEV)

What happiness for those whose guilt has been forgiven! What joys when sins are covered over! What relief for those who have confessed their sins and God has cleared their record. There was a time when I wouldn't admit what a sinner I was. But my dishonesty made me miserable and filled my days with frustration. All day and all night your hand was heavy on me. My strength evaporated like water on a sunny day until I finally admitted all my sins to you and stopped trying to hide them. I said to myself, "I will confess them to the Lord." And you forgave me! All my guilt is gone.
PSALM 32:1–5 (TLB)

Step 7: I release _____ .

The Prayer of Release—*". . . as we forgive those who sin against us."*

Forgiveness isn't about fairness. Forgiveness is about grace. The first key to learning how to forgive others is to remember how much you have been forgiven.

Be kind and tender-hearted to one another, and forgive one another,
as God has forgiven you through Christ.
EPHESIANS 4:32 (GNT)

You will never have to forgive anyone more than God has already
forgiven you.

"If you forgive those who sin against you, your heavenly Father will
forgive you. But if you refuse to forgive others, your Father will not
forgive your sins."
MATTHEW 6:14–15 (NLT)

When you are hurt, you have only two options: You can either relive it or
release it. Reliving the hurt only perpetuates the pain. But releasing the
hurt is the path to inner peace.

"Blessed are the merciful, for they will be shown mercy."
MATTHEW 5:7 (NIV)

"[Love] keeps no record of wrongs."
1 CORINTHIANS 13:5 (NIV)

Step 8: I ask God _____ .

The Prayer of Protection—*"Lead us not into temptation."*

Temptation is not always about doing the wrong thing. Temptation is
also about *not* doing the right thing.

Whatever you do, work at it with all your heart, as working for the
Lord, not for men . . . It is the Lord Christ you are serving.
COLOSSIANS 3:23–24 (NIV)

Step 9: I depend _____ .

The Prayer of Deliverance—*"Deliver us from evil."*

Step 10: I praise God _____ .

The Prayer of Victory— *"Yours is the kingdom and the power
and the glory forever. Amen."*

The Lord's Prayer ends where it begins—with the glory of God. Jesus is teaching us that the ultimate aim of our prayers is that God will be glorified, no matter the outcome. The purpose for prayer is not to conform God to my way of seeing things; the purpose for prayer is to conform me to the kingdom, power, and glory of God.

*Not to us, O Lord, not to us but to your name be the glory,
because of your love and faithfulness.*
PSALM 115:1 (NIV)

*"Our Father in heaven, hallowed be your name. Your kingdom
come. Your will be done on earth as it is in heaven. Give us this
day our daily bread. And forgive us our sins, as we forgive those
who sin against us. And lead us not into temptation, but deliver us
from evil. For yours is the kingdom and the power and the glory
forever. Amen."*
MATTHEW 6:9–13

Discovery Questions

Choose the questions that are right for your group and take time to let God work in your lives.

- **Read the verses under step six above. Why does God want us to confess our sins to him?**

_____

_____

_____

- **Pastor Rick said, "Forgiveness isn't about fairness; forgiveness is about grace. You will never have to forgive anyone more than God has forgiven you." Where would you be without God's grace? How does this truth encourage you to be more forgiving?**

_____

_____

_____

- **The goal of our prayers is to glorify God. Share some of the ways you can do this in your daily prayer life.**

_____

_____

_____

Putting It Into Practice

Be doers of the Word by applying the things you are learning. If your group is co-ed, consider breaking into subgroups by gender this week during your prayer time. This can encourage openness and can be especially helpful during this section as you share prayer requests and talk about the practice of forgiveness.

IN YOUR GROUP
PRAY TOGETHER

Before you begin praying as a group, share your individual prayer requests based on what stood out to you as an area of growth in this session: admit my faults, release others, guard my heart, depend on God's power, and praise God.

NOTES:

_____

_____

_____

_____

_____

_____

_____

IN YOUR LIFE
PRAYER OF FORGIVENESS &
TOOLS FOR TEMPTATION

If you feel bitterness, anger, or other negative emotions toward anyone, turn to A Prayer of Forgiveness on page 182 of this study guide. Use this prayer as a model to help you let go of unforgiveness. If the memory comes back and you struggle with unforgiveness again, repeat this prayer as often as necessary. Trust God every day to give you his power to forgive.

If you need help in your struggle with temptation, read the Seven Steps to Escape Temptation on page 183.

NOTES:

_____

_____

_____

_____

_____

_____

_____

_____

Daily Prayer Journal

Starting on page 102 you will find
Bible verses and daily prayer journal
prompts for The Pattern for Prayer
(Part Two). Take a few minutes every
day to read each verse several times,
slowly. Emphasize a different word or
phrase each time you read the passage.
Underline key words or phrases that are
especially meaningful to you. Follow the
prompts and write down your responses
in the journal space provided. Finish
with a prayer.

NOTES:

_____

_____

_____

_____

_____

_____

_____

_____

_____

_____

_____

_____

_____

_____

_____

_____

_____

_____

_____

_____

Daily
Prayer
Journal

"Our Father in heaven, hallowed be your name. Your kingdom come. Your will be done on earth as it is in heaven. Give us this day our daily bread. And forgive us our sins, as we forgive those who sin against us. And lead us not into temptation, but deliver us from evil. For yours is the kingdom and the power and the glory forever. Amen."

MATTHEW 6:9–13

Day 22

What did you hear?

What did God say to you as you read today's Bible passage?
What word or phrase was most meaningful to you?

_____

_____

_____

_____

What do you think?

What does this passage mean to you? How does it apply to your life?

_____

_____

_____

_____

What is your prayer?

This is where you turn your thoughts into prayer. It could be a prayer of gratitude or praise. It could be a prayer of confession or a request for God's help. It's up to you. But take a minute to write a prayer of response to God.

_____

_____

_____

_____

If we confess our sins to God, he can always be trusted to forgive us and take our sins away.

1 JOHN 1:9 (CEV)

Day 23

What did you hear?

What did God say to you as you read today's Bible passage?
What word or phrase was most meaningful to you?

_____

_____

_____

_____

What do you think?

What does this passage mean to you? How does it apply to your life?

_____

_____

_____

_____

What is your prayer?

This is where you turn your thoughts into prayer. It could be a prayer of gratitude or
praise. It could be a prayer of confession or a request for God's help. It's up to you.
But take a minute to write a prayer of response to God.

_____

_____

_____

_____

What happiness for those whose guilt has been forgiven! What joys when sins are covered over! What relief for those who have confessed their sins and God has cleared their record. There was a time when I wouldn't admit what a sinner I was. But my dishonesty made me miserable and filled my days with frustration. All day and all night your hand was heavy on me. My strength evaporated like water on a sunny day until I finally admitted all my sins to you and stopped trying to hide them. I said to myself, "I will confess them to the Lord." And you forgave me! All my guilt is gone.

PSALM 32:1–5 (TLB)

Day 24

What did you hear?

What did God say to you as you read today's Bible passage?
What word or phrase was most meaningful to you?

_____

_____

_____

_____

What do you think?

What does this passage mean to you? How does it apply to your life?

_____

_____

_____

_____

What is your prayer?

This is where you turn your thoughts into prayer. It could be a prayer of gratitude or praise. It could be a prayer of confession or a request for God's help. It's up to you. But take a minute to write a prayer of response to God.

_____

_____

_____

_____

Be kind and tender-hearted to one another, and forgive one another, as God has forgiven you through Christ.

EPHESIANS 4:32 (GNT)

Day 25

What did you hear?

What did God say to you as you read today's Bible passage?
What word or phrase was most meaningful to you?

_____

_____

_____

_____

What do you think?

What does this passage mean to you? How does it apply to your life?

_____

_____

_____

_____

What is your prayer?

This is where you turn your thoughts into prayer. It could be a prayer of gratitude or
praise. It could be a prayer of confession or a request for God's help. It's up to you.
But take a minute to write a prayer of response to God.

_____

_____

_____

_____

[Love] keeps no record of wrongs.

1 CORINTHIANS 13:5 (NIV)

Day 26

What did you hear?

What did God say to you as you read today's Bible passage?
What word or phrase was most meaningful to you?

_____

_____

_____

_____

What do you think?

What does this passage mean to you? How does it apply to your life?

_____

_____

_____

_____

What is your prayer?

This is where you turn your thoughts into prayer. It could be a prayer of gratitude or
praise. It could be a prayer of confession or a request for God's help. It's up to you.
But take a minute to write a prayer of response to God.

_____

_____

_____

_____

Whatever you do, work at it with all your heart, as working for the Lord, not for men . . . It is the Lord Christ you are serving.

COLOSSIANS 3:23–24 (NIV)

Day 27

What did you hear?

What did God say to you as you read today's Bible passage?
What word or phrase was most meaningful to you?

_____

_____

_____

_____

What do you think?

What does this passage mean to you? How does it apply to your life?

_____

_____

_____

_____

What is your prayer?

This is where you turn your thoughts into prayer. It could be a prayer of gratitude or praise. It could be a prayer of confession or a request for God's help. It's up to you. But take a minute to write a prayer of response to God.

_____

_____

_____

_____

Not to us, O Lord, not to us but to your name be the glory; because of your love and faithfulness.

PSALM 115:1 (NIV)

Day 28

What did you hear?

What did God say to you as you read today's Bible passage?
What word or phrase was most meaningful to you?

_____

_____

_____

_____

What do you think?

What does this passage mean to you? How does it apply to your life?

_____

_____

_____

_____

What is your prayer?

This is where you turn your thoughts into prayer. It could be a prayer of gratitude or praise. It could be a prayer of confession or a request for God's help. It's up to you. But take a minute to write a prayer of response to God.

_____

_____

_____

_____

Week
Five

Weekend
Sermon Notes

_____

_____

_____

_____

_____

_____

_____

_____

_____

_____

_____

_____

_____

_____

_____

_____

_____

_____

SESSION FIVE

PRAYING FOR A BREAKTHROUGH

CHECKING IN

What changes have you noticed in your prayer life at this point in our study?

KEY VERSE

*"You will seek me and find me when you
seek me with all your heart."*
JEREMIAH 29:13 (NIV)

Watch the video lesson now and follow along in your outline.

PRAYING FOR A BREAKTHROUGH

SIX STEPS FOR PRAYING FOR A BREAKTHROUGH

- Let God _____ .

During the first year of [Darius'] reign, I, Daniel, was studying the writings of [Scripture]. I learned from the word of the Lord, as recorded by Jeremiah the prophet, that Jerusalem must lie desolate for seventy years.
DANIEL 9:2 (NLT)

"If you stay connected to me and my words remain in your heart, you may ask any request you want in prayer, and it will be given to you."
JOHN 15:7

The more you fill your mind with Scripture, the more your prayers will be answered, because you will be praying according to the Word of God.

- Focus _____ .

I gave my attention to the Lord to seek him by prayer . . .
DANIEL 9:3 (NASB)

"I love those who love me, and those who seek me diligently will find me."
PROVERBS 8:17 (NKJV)

"You will seek me and find me when you seek me
with all your heart."
JEREMIAH 29:13 (NIV)

[God] rewards those who earnestly seek him.
HEBREWS 11:6 (NIV)

- Express _____ .

I prayed earnestly to the Lord, pleading with him.
DANIEL 9:3 (GNT)

I poured out my heart, baring my soul to God.
DANIEL 9:4 (THE MESSAGE)

- Demonstrate _____ .

I did not eat any food. And to show my sadness, I put on sack cloth
and sat in ashes.
DANIEL 9:3 (NCV)

- Thank God _____ .

I prayed to the Lord my God and confessed: "O Lord, you are
a great and awesome God! You always fulfill your promises of
unfailing love to those who love you and keep your commands."
DANIEL 9:4 (NLT)

Lord God, you are merciful and forgiving, even though we have
rebelled against you.
DANIEL 9:9 (CEV)

- **Humbly** _____ .

But we have sinned terribly by rebelling against you and rejecting your laws and teachings. We have ignored the message your servants the prophets spoke to [us] . . . We have been unfaithful, and have sinned against you . . . We have rebelled against you and rejected your teachings.
DANIEL 9:5–10 (CEV)

O my God, listen to me and hear my request . . . We do not ask because we deserve help, but because you are so merciful.
DANIEL 9:18 (NLT)

While I kept on praying and confessing my sin and the sins of my people, and pleading with the Lord, suddenly the angel Gabriel appeared in my vision and said to me, "Daniel, I've been sent to help you understand God's plan. The moment you began praying, an answer was given, and I'm here to tell it to you, for God loves you very much."
DANIEL 9:20–23

Discovery Questions

Choose the questions that are right for your group and take time to let God work in your lives.

- **Daniel waited seventy years for his breakthrough. How do you identify with Daniel's story? Have you ever had to pray for months or even years for a breakthrough? What was the outcome?**

_____

_____

_____

- **What is the breakthrough prayer you are asking God about right now?**

_____

_____

_____

- **Jeremiah 29:13 (NIV) says,** _"You will seek me and find me when you seek me with all your heart."_ **What does it mean to you to seek the Lord with all your heart?**

_____

_____

_____

Putting It
Into Practice

Be doers of the Word by applying the things you are learning.

IN YOUR GROUP
PRAY TOGETHER

Turn to Our Prayers & Praise on page 204 and write down each other's breakthrough prayer requests. Pray for those requests now.

Commit to praying for each other every day this week. Let people know you've prayed for them with a quick phone call, text message, or handwritten note.

NOTES:

IN YOUR LIFE
THE IMPORTANCE
OF FASTING

Have you ever fasted while praying and waiting for a breakthrough? Take a few minutes, as a group or on your own, to read the Fasting Guide on page 186. What breakthrough do you want to fast about this week? It can be your prayer or the prayer of someone in your group. What kind of fast will you commit to: a biblical fast—going without food for a period of time—or a fast from something that distracts you from your relationship with God—like electronics (phone, movies, social media), working overtime, or an over-committed social calendar? Decide on a specific date to fast this week. Get it on your calendar.

NOTES:

_____

_____

_____

_____

_____

_____

_____

Daily Prayer Journal

Starting on page 128 you will find Bible verses and daily prayer journal prompts for Praying for a Breakthrough. Take a few minutes every day to read each verse several times, slowly. Emphasize a different word or phrase each time you read the passage. Underline key words or phrases that are especially meaningful to you. Follow the prompts and write down your responses in the journal space provided. Finish with a prayer.

Before You Go

What decisions do you need to make as a group about your next small group study?

There are only two weeks left in the study, so start to talk about next-step options for your group. Be sure to plan an additional group meeting just for fellowship and to celebrate all that God is doing in your lives. Then think about what kind of study you will do you next. We encourage you to continue to explore the power of prayer as a group through the new prayer guide, *Experience God's Power Through Prayer*, available at PastorRick.com

Daily
Prayer
Journal

"You will seek me and find me when you seek me with all your heart."

JEREMIAH 29:13 (NIV)

Day 29

What did you hear?

What did God say to you as you read today's Bible passage?
What word or phrase was most meaningful to you?

_____

_____

_____

_____

What do you think?

What does this passage mean to you? How does it apply to your life?

_____

_____

_____

_____

What is your prayer?

This is where you turn your thoughts into prayer. It could be a prayer of gratitude or praise. It could be a prayer of confession or a request for God's help. It's up to you. But take a minute to write a prayer of response to God.

_____

_____

_____

_____

"If you stay connected to me and my words remain in your heart, you may ask any request you want in prayer, and it will be given to you."

JOHN 15:7

Day 30

What did you hear?

What did God say to you as you read today's Bible passage?
What word or phrase was most meaningful to you?

_____

_____

_____

_____

What do you think?

What does this passage mean to you? How does it apply to your life?

_____

_____

_____

_____

What is your prayer?

This is where you turn your thoughts into prayer. It could be a prayer of gratitude or praise. It could be a prayer of confession or a request for God's help. It's up to you. But take a minute to write a prayer of response to God.

_____

_____

_____

_____

"*I love those who love me, and those who seek me diligently will find me.*"

PROVERBS 8:17 (NKJV)

Day 31

What did you hear?

What did God say to you as you read today's Bible passage?
What word or phrase was most meaningful to you?

_____

_____

_____

_____

What do you think?

What does this passage mean to you? How does it apply to your life?

_____

_____

_____

_____

What is your prayer?

This is where you turn your thoughts into prayer. It could be a prayer of gratitude or
praise. It could be a prayer of confession or a request for God's help. It's up to you.
But take a minute to write a prayer of response to God.

_____

_____

_____

_____

*I prayed to the Lord my God and
confessed: "O Lord, you are
a great and awesome God!
You always fulfill your promises
of unfailing love to those who love
you and keep your commands."*

DANIEL 9:4 (NLT)

Day 32

What did you hear?

What did God say to you as you read today's Bible passage?
What word or phrase was most meaningful to you?

_____

_____

_____

_____

What do you think?

What does this passage mean to you? How does it apply to your life?

_____

_____

_____

_____

What is your prayer?

This is where you turn your thoughts into prayer. It could be a prayer of gratitude or
praise. It could be a prayer of confession or a request for God's help. It's up to you.
But take a minute to write a prayer of response to God.

_____

_____

_____

_____

"Lord God, you are merciful and forgiving, even though we have rebelled against you."

DANIEL 9:9 (CEV)

Day 33

What did you hear?

What did God say to you as you read today's Bible passage?
What word or phrase was most meaningful to you?

_____

_____

_____

_____

What do you think?

What does this passage mean to you? How does it apply to your life?

_____

_____

_____

_____

What is your prayer?

This is where you turn your thoughts into prayer. It could be a prayer of gratitude or
praise. It could be a prayer of confession or a request for God's help. It's up to you.
But take a minute to write a prayer of response to God.

_____

_____

_____

_____

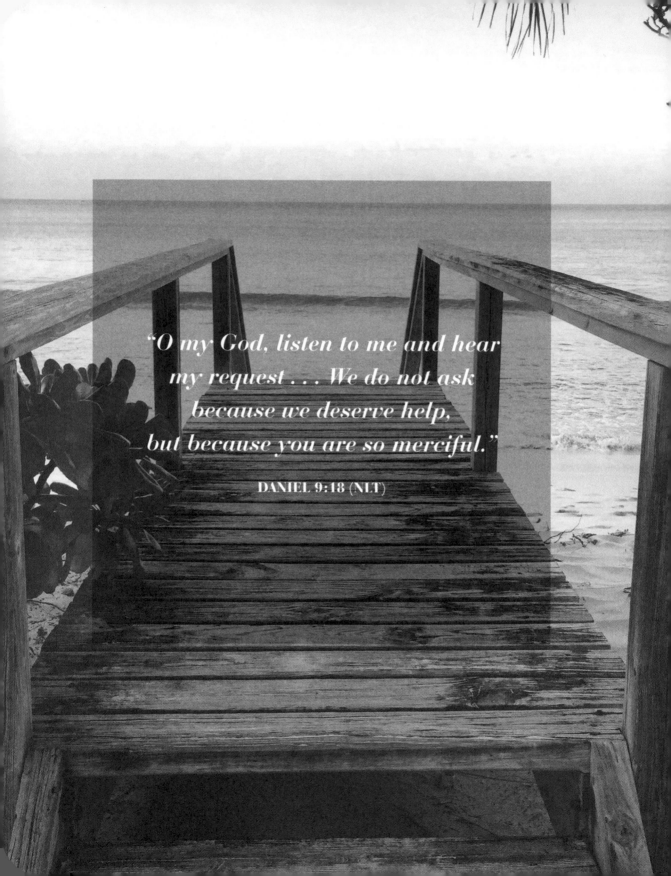

"O my God, listen to me and hear my request . . . We do not ask because we deserve help, but because you are so merciful."

DANIEL 9:18 (NLT)

Day 34

What did you hear?

What did God say to you as you read today's Bible passage?
What word or phrase was most meaningful to you?

_____

_____

_____

_____

What do you think?

What does this passage mean to you? How does it apply to your life?

_____

_____

_____

_____

What is your prayer?

This is where you turn your thoughts into prayer. It could be a prayer of gratitude or praise. It could be a prayer of confession or a request for God's help. It's up to you. But take a minute to write a prayer of response to God.

_____

_____

_____

_____

While I kept on praying and confessing my sin and the sins of my people, and pleading with the Lord, suddenly the angel Gabriel appeared in my vision and said to me, "Daniel, I've been sent to help you understand God's plan. The moment you began praying, an answer was given, and I'm here to tell it to you, for God loves you very much."

DANIEL 9:20–23

Day 35

What did you hear?

What did God say to you as you read today's Bible passage?
What word or phrase was most meaningful to you?

_____

_____

_____

_____

What do you think?

What does this passage mean to you? How does it apply to your life?

_____

_____

_____

_____

What is your prayer?

This is where you turn your thoughts into prayer. It could be a prayer of gratitude or praise. It could be a prayer of confession or a request for God's help. It's up to you. But take a minute to write a prayer of response to God.

_____

_____

_____

_____

Week
Six

Weekend
Sermon Notes

_____

_____

_____

_____

_____

_____

_____

_____

_____

_____

_____

_____

_____

_____

_____

_____

_____

_____

HOW TO PRAY IN A CRISIS

CHECKING IN

Does anyone have an update on their breakthrough prayer from last session? Or for those of you who had the opportunity to fast, share what that experience was like for you.

KEY VERSE

"Do not be afraid or discouraged . . .
For the battle is not yours, but God's."
2 CHRONICLES 20:15 (NIV)

Watch the video lesson now and follow along in your outline.

HOW TO PRAY IN A CRISIS

Messengers came and told Jehoshaphat, "A vast army from Edom is marching against you from beyond the Dead Sea. They are already [about two days away]" . . . Jehoshaphat was terrified by this news.
2 CHRONICLES 20:2–3 (NLT)

SIX LESSONS FROM KING JEHOSHAPHAT

- Turn to _____ .

Jehoshaphat was terrified by this news and begged the Lord for guidance. He also ordered everyone in Judah to begin fasting.
2 CHRONICLES 20:3 (NLT)

Never let a problem intimidate you. Instead, let it motivate you to pray! Seek God for wisdom before you do anything else.

- ○ Remember _____ .

"O Lord, God of our fathers, <u>are you not</u> the God who is in heaven? You rule over all the kingdoms of the nations. Power and might are in your hand, and no one can withstand you."
2 CHRONICLES 20:6 (NIV)

- ○ Remember _____ .

"O God, <u>did you not</u> drive out the inhabitants of this land before your people Israel?"
2 CHRONICLES 20:7 (NIV)

- Remember _____ .

*"__Did you not__ . . . give [this land] forever to the descendants of
Abraham your friend?"*
2 CHRONICLES 20:7 (NIV)

- Appeal _____ .

*"You would not allow us to invade their territory when we came
up from Egypt; so we turned away from them and did not destroy
them. See how they are repaying us . . . O our God, __will you not__
__judge them?__"*
2 CHRONICLES 20:10–12

In essence, Jehoshaphat said to God, "I know who you are, I know what you
have done, I know what you have said, and I know what you can do—and I'm
asking you to do it again!"

- Admit _____ .

*"We have no power to face this vast army that is attacking us.
We do not know what to do . . ."*
2 CHRONICLES 20:12 (NIV)

Miracles never happen until you admit that the situation is impossible
without God's help.

"With man, this is impossible, but with God all things are possible."
MATTHEW 19:26 (NIV)

- Rely _____ .

"We do not know what to do, but our eyes are upon you."
2 CHRONICLES 20:12 NIV)

Shift your focus from your problem to the Problem Solver.

- **Relax** _____.

"Do not be afraid or discouraged because of this vast army. For the battle is not yours, but God's . . . You will not have to fight this battle. Take up your positions; stand firm and see the deliverance the Lord will give you. Do not be afraid; do not be discouraged."
2 CHRONICLES 20:15, 17 (NIV)

When you put your life in God's hands, your battles become his battles, and your enemies become his enemies. And God says to you, just like he said to Jehoshaphat, "Relax. I've got this."

"Have faith in the Lord your God, and you will stand strong. Have faith in his prophets, and you will succeed."
2 CHRONICLES 20:20 (NCV)

- **Thank God** _____.

Sing victory songs before you see the victory!

Jehoshaphat appointed men to sing to the Lord and to praise him for the splendor of his holiness as they went out at the head of the army, saying: "Give thanks to the Lord, for his love endures forever."
2 CHRONICLES 20:21 (NIV)

Thank God for what he is going to do, even though you don't know how he is going to do it. If you thank God after the fact, that's gratitude. But if you thank God in advance, that's faith.

Without faith it is impossible to please God, because anyone who comes to him must believe that he exists and that he rewards those who earnestly seek him.
HEBREWS 11:6 (NIV)

At the moment they began to sing and to praise, the Lord caused the armies of Ammon, Moab, and Mount Seir to begin fighting among themselves, and they destroyed each other!
2 CHRONICLES 20:22 (TLB)

The Israelites didn't run in fear; they stood firm in their faith. They didn't have to lift a finger; they just lifted their voices in worship, and their enemies self-destructed. There is power in praise!

- **Expect God** _____ .

Not a single one of the enemy had escaped. King Jehoshaphat and his men went out to gather the plunder. They found vast amounts of equipment, clothing, and other valuables—more than they could carry. There was so much plunder that it took them three days just to collect it all! On the fourth day they gathered in the Valley of Blessing, which got its name that day because the people praised and thanked the Lord there. It is still called the Valley of Blessing today.
2 CHRONICLES 20:24–26 (NLT)

When you let God fight your battles, it is a witness to everyone around you.

When all the surrounding kingdoms heard that the Lord himself had fought against the enemies of Israel, the fear of God came over them. So Jehoshaphat's kingdom was at peace, for his God had given him rest on every side.
2 CHRONICLES 20:29–30 (NLT)

Discovery
Questions

Choose the questions that are right for your group and take time to let God work in your lives.

- Has there ever been a time when you stopped to praise and thank God first in a moment of crisis? If so, how did that act of faith impact your perspective on the crisis? What changes did you experience physically, emotionally and mentally—were you less anxious or worried, etc.?

  _____

  _____

  _____

- Jehoshaphat prayed, *"We do not know what to do, but our eyes are upon you"* (2 Chronicles 20:12 NIV). Is there a situation that is overwhelming or intimidating you? What steps can you take to shift your focus from your problem to the Problem Solver?

  _____

  _____

  _____

- Pastor Rick said, "When you let God fight your battles, it is a witness to everyone around you." What are you communicating to the people around you by the way you handle the crises in your life? What does it say about your faith?

  _____

  _____

  _____

Putting It Into Practice

Be doers of the Word by applying the things you are learning.

PRAY TOGETHER

Jehoshaphat didn't try to handle his crisis alone, and neither should you. If anyone is in crisis, or in need of a big breakthrough right now, gather around them, place your hands on their shoulders, and pray for them. Close your time together by giving thanks as a group—thanking God for his presence and for his victory in your lives.

PRAY THE PLAN

If you or someone you know is going through a crisis, use Jehoshaphat's model of prayer this week.

1. **Turn to God for help with these three reminders: Are you not, did you not, will you not?**

2. **Admit your inadequacy.**

3. **Rely on God's resources.**

4. **Relax in faith.**

5. **Thank God in advance for hearing and answering your prayer.**

6. **Expect God to turn your battle into blessings.**

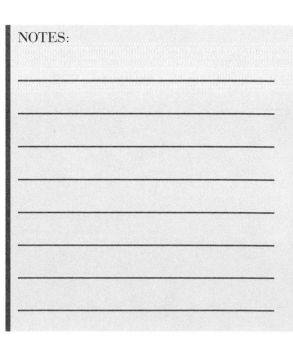

NOTES:

_____

_____

_____

_____

_____

_____

_____

Daily Prayer Journal

Starting on page 154 you will find Bible verses and daily prayer journal prompts for Praying for a Breakthrough. Take a few minutes every day to read each verse several times, slowly. Emphasize a different word or phrase each time you read the passage. Underline key words or phrases that are especially meaningful to you. Follow the prompts and write down your responses in the journal space provided. Finish with a prayer.

Before You Go

What decisions do you need to make as a group this week?

- **WRITE TO RICK!** Pastor Rick would love to hear your story of what 40 Days of Prayer has meant to you. You can write to him at **Rick@PastorRick.com.**

- **EXPLORE RESOURCES!** Visit **PastorRick.com** and check out these great resources:

  ○ You will find dozens of video-based small group studies.

  ○ You can order your copy of Pastor Rick's *Experience God's Power Through Prayer* guide.

  ○ You can learn about Pastor Rick's daily teaching program, *Daily Hope,* available on radio, internet, and podcast.

  ○ You can also sign up to receive *Daily Hope* devotions, delivered directly to your email inbox every day. They're absolutely free!

- **PLAN A PARTY!** Have you made plans for a party with your group to celebrate what God has done in your lives through this study of 40 Days of Prayer? A party is an excellent opportunity for you to invite new people who might be interested in joining your group. Talk about your celebration before you leave your meeting. Where will you have your party? When will you have it? Will it be a potluck or a barbecue, or will you call out for pizza? Divide up the responsibilities and get ready to enjoy a great time of fellowship.

Daily
Prayer
Journal

"O Lord, God of our fathers, are you not the God who is in heaven? You rule over all the kingdoms of the nations. Power and might are in your hand, and no one can withstand you."

2 CHRONICLES 20:6 (NIV)

Day 36

What did you hear?

What did God say to you as you read today's Bible passage?
What word or phrase was most meaningful to you?

_____

_____

_____

_____

What do you think?

What does this passage mean to you? How does it apply to your life?

_____

_____

_____

_____

What is your prayer?

This is where you turn your thoughts into prayer. It could be a prayer of gratitude or
praise. It could be a prayer of confession or a request for God's help. It's up to you.
But take a minute to write a prayer of response to God.

_____

_____

_____

_____

"*Our God, did you not drive out the inhabitants of this land before your people Israel and give it forever to the descendants of Abraham your friend? They have lived in it and have built in it a sanctuary for your Name, saying, 'If calamity comes upon us, whether the sword of judgment, or plague or famine, we will stand in your presence before this temple that bears your Name and will cry out to you in our distress, and you will hear us and save us.'*"

2 CHRONICLES 20:7–9 (NIV)

Day 37

What did you hear?

What did God say to you as you read today's Bible passage?
What word or phrase was most meaningful to you?

_____

_____

_____

_____

What do you think?

What does this passage mean to you? How does it apply to your life?

_____

_____

_____

_____

What is your prayer?

This is where you turn your thoughts into prayer. It could be a prayer of gratitude or praise. It could be a prayer of confession or a request for God's help. It's up to you. But take a minute to write a prayer of response to God.

_____

_____

_____

_____

"You would not allow us to invade their territory when we came up from Egypt; so we turned away from them and did not destroy them. See how they are repaying us . . . O our God, will you not judge them? For we have no power to face this vast army that is attacking us. We do not know what to do, but our eyes are on you."

2 CHRONICLES 20:10–12

Day 38

What did you hear?

What did God say to you as you read today's Bible passage?
What word or phrase was most meaningful to you?

_____

_____

_____

_____

What do you think?

What does this passage mean to you? How does it apply to your life?

_____

_____

_____

_____

What is your prayer?

This is where you turn your thoughts into prayer. It could be a prayer of gratitude or
praise. It could be a prayer of confession or a request for God's help. It's up to you.
But take a minute to write a prayer of response to God.

_____

_____

_____

_____

"Do not be afraid or discouraged because of this vast army. For the battle is not yours, but God's . . . You will not have to fight this battle. Take up your positions; stand firm and see the deliverance the Lord will give you . . . Do not be afraid; do not be discouraged."

2 CHRONICLES 20:15–17 (NIV)

Day 39

What did you hear?

What did God say to you as you read today's Bible passage?
What word or phrase was most meaningful to you?

_____

_____

_____

_____

What do you think?

What does this passage mean to you? How does it apply to your life?

_____

_____

_____

_____

What is your prayer?

This is where you turn your thoughts into prayer. It could be a prayer of gratitude or
praise. It could be a prayer of confession or a request for God's help. It's up to you.
But take a minute to write a prayer of response to God.

_____

_____

_____

_____

Without faith it is impossible to please God, because anyone who comes to him must believe that he exists and that he rewards those who earnestly seek him.

HEBREWS 11:6 (NIV)

Day 40

What did you hear?

What did God say to you as you read today's Bible passage?
What word or phrase was most meaningful to you?

_____

_____

_____

_____

What do you think?

What does this passage mean to you? How does it apply to your life?

_____

_____

_____

_____

What is your prayer?

This is where you turn your thoughts into prayer. It could be a prayer of gratitude or
praise. It could be a prayer of confession or a request for God's help. It's up to you.
But take a minute to write a prayer of response to God.

_____

_____

_____

_____

Bonus
Session

Weekend
Sermon Notes

_____

_____

_____

_____

_____

_____

_____

_____

_____

_____

_____

_____

_____

_____

_____

_____

_____

_____

_____

WHY DOESN'T GOD ALWAYS ANSWER THE FIRST TIME I PRAY?

CHECKING IN

What opportunities have you had this week to pray with someone going through a crisis or encourage someone who is feeling overwhelmed?

KEY VERSE

Always keep on praying.
1 THESSALONIANS 5:17 (TLB)

Watch the video lesson now and follow along in your outline.

WHY DOESN'T GOD ALWAYS ANSWER THE FIRST TIME I PRAY?

"Ask and it will be given to you; seek and you will find;
knock and the door will be opened to you."
LUKE 11:9 (NIV)

"For everyone who asks [and keeps on asking] receives; the one who
seeks [and keeps on seeking] finds; and to the one who knocks
[and keeps on knocking], the door will be opened."
LUKE 11:10 (NIV)

Be persistent in prayer, and keep alert as you pray;
giving thanks to God.
COLOSSIANS 4:2 (GNT)

WHY DOES GOD WANT ME TO PERSIST IN PRAYER?

- **Praying persistently** _____ .

My eyes are always looking to the Lord for help.
PSALM 25:15 (NCV)

Look to the Lord and his strength; seek his face always.
PSALM 105:4 (NIV)

- Praying persistently _____.

While you are working on your prayer, God is working on you.

"I will test . . . and will purify them as silver is purified by fire. I will test them as gold is tested. Then they will pray to me, and I will answer them."
ZECHARIAH 13:9 (GNT)

- God will _____ me before he _____ me.

- Praying persistently _____ _____ _____

"The thing you should want most is God's kingdom and doing what God wants. Then all these other things you need will be given to you."
MATTHEW 6:33 (NCV)

Take delight in the Lord, and he will give you the desires of your heart.
PSALM 37:4 (NRSV)

- Praying persistently _____.

- _____ is a mark of maturity.

God left [Hezekiah] on his own to see what he would do; [God] wanted to test his heart."
2 CHRONICLES 32:31 (THE MESSAGE)

The first question you have to ask yourself is, "Am I willing to let God change me instead of changing the circumstance?"

Give yourselves completely to God . . . to be tools in the hands of
God, to be used for his good purposes.
ROMANS 6:13 (TLB)

- **Praying persistently** _____ .

Ultimately, the real question you have to answer is: Do I trust my feelings,
or do I trust my Father? Will I trust him even if his answer isn't what I
had in mind?

- ◦ When _____ , God says _____ .

- ◦ When _____ , God says _____ .

- ◦ When _____ , God says _____ .

"These things I plan won't happen right away. Slowly, steadily,
surely, the time approaches when the vision will be fulfilled. If it
seems slow, do not despair, for these things will surely come to pass.
Just be patient! They will not be overdue a single day!"
HABAKKUK 2:3 (TLB)

- ◦ When _____

    are all lined up, God says _____ .

Always keep on praying.
1 THESSALONIANS 5:17 (TLB)

Let us not get tired of doing what is right, for after a while we will
reap a harvest of blessing if we don't get discouraged and give up.
GALATIANS 6:9 (TLB)

Discovery Questions

Choose the questions that are right for your group and take time to let God work in your lives.

- **Praying persistently teaches us about ourselves. What do you think God is trying to teach you as you wait for him to answer your prayer?**

_____

_____

_____

- **Praying persistently tests our faith. Using the model of "no, grow, slow, and go," in what ways has your faith been tested as you persist in prayer?**

_____

_____

_____

- **What has been the greatest highlight or takeaway for you during 40 Days of Prayer?**

_____

_____

_____

Putting It Into Practice

Be doers of the Word by applying the things you are learning.

IN YOUR GROUP
PRAY & GIVE THANKS

The Bible says, *"As for me, I will certainly not sin against the Lord by ending my prayers for you"* (1 Samuel 12:23 NLT). So let's not end our prayers for one another! Let's put this biblical truth into practice. Write your persistent prayer request on a card, and exchange your cards in whatever manner works best for your group—you could also text your prayer request to another group member. Make a commitment to check in with each other this week regarding these requests. Spend time praying as a group, giving thanks to God for his goodness over the last 40 days.

IN YOUR LIFE
THE HAND PRAYER

Could you use some help organizing your thoughts in prayer? Turn to page 188 and pray through The Hand Prayer model. Practice this prayer model throughout the week. We hope you will make a lifelong commitment to deepening your prayer life. It's the best way to strengthen your friendship with God.

Also, be sure to check out Ten Great Books on Prayer on page 190.

Consider joining the prayer ministry team at your church. Check with your small group leader or pastor to find out if there is a prayer ministry at your church. This would be a great way to serve others and continue deepening your prayer life. If your church doesn't have a prayer ministry, pray and ask God if he wants you to start one!

Before You Go

- **WRITE TO RICK!** Pastor Rick would love to hear your story of what 40 Days of Prayer has meant to you. You can write to him at **Rick@PastorRick.com.**

- **EXPLORE RESOURCES!** Visit **PastorRick.com** and check out these great resources:

  ○ You will find dozens of video-based small group studies.

  ○ You can order your copy of Pastor Rick's *Experience God's Power Through Prayer* guide.

  ○ You can learn about Pastor Rick's daily teaching program, *Daily Hope*, available on radio, internet, and podcast.

  ○ You can also sign up to receive *Daily Hope* devotions, delivered directly to your email inbox every day. They're absolutely free!

- **PLAN A PARTY!** Have you made plans for a party with your group to celebrate what God has done in your lives through this study of 40 Days of Prayer? A party is an excellent opportunity for you to invite new people who might be interested in joining your group. Talk about your celebration before you leave your meeting. Where will you have your party? When will you have it? Will it be a potluck or a barbecue, or will you call out for pizza? Divide up the responsibilities and get ready to enjoy a great time of fellowship.

PRAYER RESOURCES

DAILY PRAYER OF SURRENDER

Praying with your palms up symbolizes that you are bringing your requests and cares to God. Turning your palms down symbolizes that you are letting go and releasing your cares into God's hands. Turning your palms up again symbolizes that you are receiving God's grace, and that your hands are now available to him to be used for his purposes.

With your palms turned up, pray:

Father, I come to you today in Jesus' name. Thank you for your kindness that has brought me to another day. Thank you for your love and faithfulness. Thank you for accepting me as I am and for transforming me into the likeness of Christ. I present myself before you—body, soul, and spirit. I bring you my strengths and my weaknesses, my hopes and my fears, my successes and my failures, my dreams and my nightmares . . . (Now take a moment to tell God what's on your mind.)

With your palms turned down, pray:

Now, Father, by faith I release all of these things into your lap of grace and I surrender to your sovereignty. I cast all of my cares upon you, and I pray, "Let your will be done in my life today . . ."

With your palms turned up, pray:

Father, I now receive from you all that your grace will afford to me today: strength for my weaknesses, peace for my fears, forgiveness for my sins, and the grace to forgive those who sin against me. I look to you to meet all of my needs. Guide my steps, direct my thoughts, and protect me from evil. I invite you to fill me today with your Holy Spirit. Let me be an extension of your grace and mercy to the world around me. Use my life, I pray, to bring glory to your name. In Jesus' name, amen.

From *The Way of a Worshiper* by Buddy Owens. Used by permission.

THE EPHESIANS 3:20 EXERCISE

> *[God] is able to do far more than we would ever dare to ask or even dream of—infinitely beyond our highest prayers, desires, thoughts, or hopes.*
> EPHESIANS 3:20 (TLB)

What did you hear?

What did God say to you as you read today's Bible passage?
What word or phrase was most meaningful to you?

_____

_____

_____

What do you think?

What does this passage mean to you? How does it apply to your life?

_____

_____

_____

What is your prayer?

This is where you turn your thoughts into prayer. It could be a prayer of gratitude or praise. It could be a prayer of confession or a request for God's help. It's up to you. But take a minute to write a prayer of response to God.

_____

_____

GRATITUDE LIST: GOD'S GOODNESS TO ME FROM A–Z

"In everything, by prayer and petition, with thanksgiving, present your requests to God."
PHILIPPIANS 4:6 (NIV)

Prayer should always start with gratitude. Use this tool to help you think alphabetically of people and things to thank God for. How has he blessed you spiritually, relationally, and materially? When you remember what God has already done for you, it builds your faith to pray again.

A

_____

B

_____

C

_____

D

_____

E

F

G

H

I

J

K

L

M

N

O

P

Q

R

S

T

_____

U

_____

V

_____

W

_____

X

_____

Y

_____

Z

_____

A PRAYER OF FORGIVENESS

Dear Lord,

I may not be able to forget, but I'm choosing to forgive

_____.

I realize trust may take time to rebuild,

but I choose to hold no grudges.

Help me to let go of bitterness or anger in my heart,

so that I may live in freedom.

Give me your grace so that I may relinquish

my "right" to get even.

Help me understand that you have forgiven me

and that I can forgive _____ through you.

I trust in your power to do that.

Now, Lord, I ask you to bless _____.

In particular, I ask you to bless them with these things:

_____.

God,

please replace my hurt with your healing.

Replace my pain with your peace.

Replace my loss with your love.

May the past truly be the past.

In Jesus' name I pray, amen.

SEVEN STEPS TO ESCAPE TEMPTATION

The temptations that come into your life are no different from what others experience. And God is faithful. He will keep the temptation from becoming so strong that you can't stand up against it. When you are tempted, he will show you a way out so that you will not give in to it.
1 CORINTHIANS 10:13 (NLT)

It is not a sin to be tempted. The Bible says Jesus was tempted just like we are, but he never sinned. God will never get angry with you when you are tempted. He wants to show you a way out. Here are seven biblical steps that will help you escape temptation.

Step 1: Get into the Word.

When Jesus was tempted, his only defense was the Word of God. He said, "It is written . . . It is written . . . It is written." You cannot say, "It is written," if you don't know what is written.

I have hidden your word in my heart that I might not sin against you.
PSALM 119:11 (NIV)

Step 2: Identify your vulnerabilities.

"Watch and pray so that you will not fall into temptation. The spirit is willing, but the body is weak."
MATTHEW 26:41 (NIV)

Notice that Jesus said it's not enough just to pray. You also have to watch. Be on your guard. Ask yourself these questions:

When am I most tempted?
What day of the week? What time of day?

Where am I most tempted?

At work? At a friend's house? At the mall? At a sports bar? Perhaps it's in the kitchen or in front of the computer. You need to be honest with yourself and admit your area of vulnerability.

Who is with me when I'm most tempted?

Am I most tempted when I'm alone? When I'm with friends who lead me in the wrong direction? When I'm with a crowd of strangers and I think nobody would know me?

How do I feel before I'm tempted?

What is the emotional trigger? Is it frustration, exhaustion, anger, stress? Is it boredom or restlessness? Is it loneliness or self-pity?

Step 3: Plan what you're not going to do.

Plan carefully what you do . . . Avoid evil and walk straight ahead. Don't go one step off the right way.
PROVERBS 4:26–27 (GNT)

Plan in advance to stay away from people, places, or circumstances that cause you to be vulnerable to temptation. If you don't want to get stung, stay away from the bees. Plan what you're *not* going to do, and then stick to your plan.

Step 4: Guard your heart.

Temptation comes from our own desires, which entice us and drag us away.
JAMES 1:14 (NLT)

Temptation is an inside job. The Devil can't make you do anything. He can try to lure you into temptation, but your actions come from your own decisions, and your decisions reflect the condition of your heart.

Above all else, guard your heart, for it affects everything you do.
PROVERBS 4:23 (NLT)

Step 5: Pray for deliverance.

The prayer of deliverance can be boiled down to just one word: Help! When your back is against the wall, when you're in over your head, when it seems everything and everyone is conspiring for your downfall, pray the prayer of deliverance. Call out to God for help.

God is faithful. He will keep the temptation from becoming so strong that you can't stand up against it. When you are tempted, he will show you a way out so that you will not give in to it.
1 CORINTHIANS 10:13 (NLT)

Step 6: Refocus your attention.

Whatever gets your attention gets you. The battle for sin always starts in your mind. The only way to win that battle and escape temptation is to change your focus and think about something else.

Do not conform any longer to the pattern of this world, but be transformed by the renewing of your mind. Then you will be able to test and approve what God's will is—his good, pleasing and perfect will.
ROMANS 12:2 (NIV)

Step 7: Find a friend.

You need a spiritual partner to live a spiritual life. If you had a trusted friend to whom you could confess your temptations, you would have fewer sins to confess to God. If you want to have that kind of friend, you must be that kind of friend.

Two are better than one because together they can work more effectively. If one of them falls down, the other can help his friend get up. But how tragic it is for the one who is all alone when he falls. There is no one to help him get up.
ECCLESIASTES 4:9–10 (GNT/GW)

FASTING GUIDE

What Is Fasting and Why Is It Important?

"Fasting is not so much about food as it is about focus. It's not so much about saying no to the body as it is about saying yes to God."
– Lance Witt

The Bible is clear that there is power in our prayers when they are coupled with fasting. Throughout history, God's people united in prayer and fasting to seek God's favor, deliverance, direction, or provision:

- Moses fasted before he received the Ten Commandments (Exodus 34:28).

- God's people fasted when they were under attack from their enemies (2 Chronicles 20:3).

- David fasted in mourning and repentance (2 Samuel 12:16).

- Ezra led the nation in prayer and fasting for protection and success in building the temple (Ezra 8:21).

- God's people fasted when Esther went before the king to win their deliverance (Esther 4:16).

- Daniel fasted and prayed for God's mercy on the nation (Daniel 9:3).

- Nehemiah fasted before beginning the rebuilding of the walls of Jerusalem (Nehemiah 1:4).

- Jesus fasted during his victory over temptation (Matthew 4:2).

- The early church fasted to receive direction in their decisions (Acts 13:2–3).

- The apostle Paul fasted when appointing leaders for the church (Acts 14:23).

Jesus not only practiced fasting, he also taught us to fast. In the middle of the Sermon of the Mount, Jesus said this:

"When you fast, do not look somber as the hypocrites do, for they disfigure their faces to show men they are fasting. I tell you the truth, they have received their reward in full. But when you fast, put oil on your head and wash your face, so that it will not be obvious to men that you are fasting, but only to your Father, who is unseen; and your Father, who sees what is done in secret, will reward you."
MATTHEW 6:16–18 (NIV)

Notice Jesus doesn't say *if* you fast. He says *when* you fast. He assumed we would do it, so he taught the proper attitude about fasting.

A biblical fast means to reduce or eliminate food intake for a specific period of time for the purpose of seeking God. The proper way to fast is to use the time you would have spent preparing, eating, and sharing a meal to feast on the Word and talk to the Lord. Think of it this way: How long would it take you to have lunch with a friend? And what would you do when you had lunch together? You would eat and talk. Think of reading the Word as the eating part of the meal, and prayer as the conversational part of the meal. Take your time. Don't eat too fast. Read the Scriptures slowly. And don't rush the conversation. Instead, enjoy God's company. Give God your full attention, and tell him why you are fasting.

There are many ways to fast. You can abstain from food and liquids for one or more days. You can fast just from food. You can do a partial fast from certain foods (sometimes called a Daniel fast). If fasting is new for you, you might just try fasting from one meal. Fast during your lunch break and use that time to "feast" on the Lord. Go out to your car, sit at your desk, or go for a walk, but use that time to read your Bible and talk to God in prayer.

Fasting is truly a way to focus on God—spirit, soul, and body.

THE HAND PRAYER

The Bible says, *"Every day I call upon you, O Lord; I spread out my hands to you"* (Psalm 88:9 ESV). Here's a way to pray using your hands.

The five fingers on your left hand represent *who* to pray for, and the five fingers on your right hand represent *what* to pray for. Once you remember these prompts, you can pray this prayer in just five minutes.

Challenge yourself to use the hand prayer for the next thirty days. It takes about thirty days to build a habit; but, once you've made it a habit, you'll do it the rest of your life.

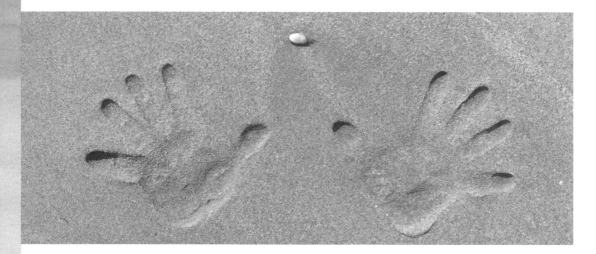

THE **LEFT HAND** TEACHES US **WHO** TO PRAY FOR

Left Thumb: If you hold your hands together in a prayer position, you'll notice that your thumbs are closest to your heart. This is a reminder to pray for those who are closest to your heart, such as family and friends.

Left Index Finger: We use the index finger to point the way, so this is a reminder to pray for those in our lives who point the way, such as teachers, pastors, and leaders.

Left Middle (Tallest) Finger: The Bible says we're to pray for the people who influence the world, such as those in authority. Our tallest finger can remind us to pray for them.

Left Ring (Fourth) Finger: Some people believe this is our weakest finger, suggesting it's difficult to hold anything with it. This can be a reminder to pray for those who need our extra support. This would include the sick, the poor, children, and the elderly—or people challenged by a handicap or a mental-health issue.

Left Small (Fifth) Finger: Finally, pray for yourself and your own needs. It's okay to pray for yourself, but by using this model, you are putting other people first.

THE RIGHT HAND TEACHES US WHAT TO PRAY FOR

Right Thumb: Once again, the thumb is closest to your heart, so pray about your heart: "God, is my heart right with you? Is there anything between you and me that is creating a barrier? Is there anything I need to confess?" You can also pray for the hearts of people around you: your family, friends, neighbors, and co-workers.

Right Index Finger: We use the index finger to point the way, so use this as a reminder to ask God about your priorities and schedule. What is most important? What should I let go of?

Right Middle (Tallest) Finger: Use this finger to remind you to pray about your influence. It's okay to ask God to give you more influence or to help you be an example to others. You can pray, "Lord, I'm getting ready to start a new day. People are going to see things in my life, and I want to be a good influence today."

Right Ring (Fourth) Finger: We refer to the fourth finger on each hand as the ring finger, so the fourth thing to pray for is relationships. Ask God to bless the people in your small group, those you work with or go to school with , and the people serving alongside you in ministry.

Right Small (Fifth) Finger: Use this finger as a reminder to pray for material blessings. There's nothing wrong with asking God to bless you materially. The Bible says, *"You can be sure that God will take care of everything you need, his generosity exceeding even yours in the glory that pours from Jesus"* (Philippians 4:19 The Message).

TEN GREAT BOOKS ON PRAYER

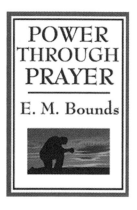

POWER THROUGH PRAYER

E. M. Bounds

Power through Prayer has been called "one of the truly great masterpieces on the theme of prayer." This small but powerful book is a classic and essential resource to improve your prayer life.

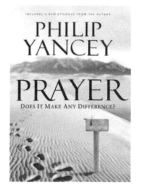

PRAYER: DOES IT MAKE ANY DIFFERENCE?

Philip Yancey

Yancey probes the very heartbeat of mankind's relationship to God in this invitation to communicate with God through prayer. *Prayer: Does It Make Any Difference?* is an exploration of the mysterious intersection where God and humans meet and relate.

PRAYER: FINDING THE HEART'S TRUE HOME
Richard Foster

Best-selling author Richard J. Foster offers a warm, compelling, and sensitive primer on prayer, helping us to understand, experience, and practice it in its many forms—from the simple prayer of beginning again to unceasing prayer.

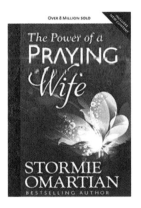

THE POWER OF A PRAYING WIFE
Stormie Omartian

Today's challenges can make a fulfilling marriage seem like an impossible dream. Yet God delights in doing the impossible if only we would ask! Stormie Omartian shares how God can strengthen your marriage as you pray for your husband concerning key areas in his life.

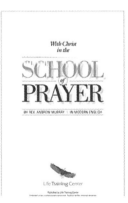

WITH CHRIST IN THE SCHOOL OF PRAYER
Andrew Murray

Immerse yourself in this timeless classic and prepare yourself for one of the most vital ministries believers can experience—intercessory prayer! Using Jesus' teaching on prayer as a model, Murray begins at the elementary level and leads you step by step through thirty-one lessons to the heights of faith-empowered prayer.

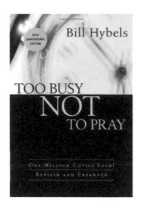

TOO BUSY NOT TO PRAY
Bill Hybels

This twentieth-anniversary edition of *Too Busy Not to Pray* calls both young and old to make prayer a priority, and broadens our vision for what our eternal, powerful God does when his people slow down to pray.

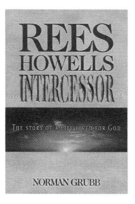

REES HOWELLS: INTERCESSOR
Norman Grubb

How did the faith and prayers of a humble coal miner affect the course of World War II? In this biography of Rees Howells, whose mastery of intercessory prayer had global consequences, we discover rich truths of the Spirit for all the church today.

PRAYER: THE GREAT ADVENTURE
David Jeremiah

Prayer: The Great Adventure gently encourages us to take the first steps toward fostering a rewarding relationship with God. With gentle, practical guidance, Dr. David Jeremiah shares his own story of learning to pray out of desperation, inspiring you to find the same urgency and intimacy in every stage of your glorious journey with God.

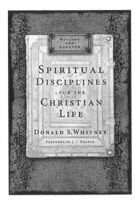

SPIRITUAL DISCIPLINES FOR THE CHRISTIAN LIFE
Donald S. Whitney

Donald Whitney's methods of Bible reading and prayer are must-reads for every believer. He writes in everyday language for everyday people.

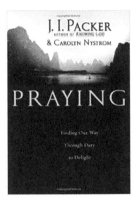

PRAYING: FINDING OUR WAY THROUGH DUTY TO DELIGHT
J. I. Packer & Carolyn Nystrom

Does prayer often seem more of a job than a joy? Packer and Nystrom's practical help for whole-person praying will move you to deeper obedience, delight, and intimacy with the Father. You'll discover different aspects of prayer, including praising, asking, brooding, complaining, and joining in!

SMALL GROUP RESOURCES

HELPS FOR HOSTS

TOP 10 IDEAS FOR NEW HOSTS

CONGRATULATIONS! As the host of your small group, you have responded to the call to help shepherd Jesus' flock. Few other tasks in the family of God surpass the contribution you will be making. As you prepare to facilitate your group, whether it is one session or the entire series, here are a few thoughts to keep in mind.

Remember you are not alone. God knows everything about you, and he knew you would be asked to facilitate your group. You may not feel ready; this is common for all good hosts. God promises, *"I will never leave you; I will never abandon you"* (Hebrews 13:5 NCV). Whether you are facilitating for one evening, several weeks, or a lifetime, you will be blessed as you serve.

1. DON'T TRY TO DO IT ALONE. Pray right now for God to help you build a healthy team. If you can enlist a co-host to help you shepherd the group, you will find your experience much richer. This is your chance to involve as many people as you can in building a healthy group. All you have to do is ask people to help. You'll be surprised at the response.

2. BE FRIENDLY AND BE YOURSELF. God wants to use your unique gifts and temperament. Be sure to greet people at the door with a big smile—this can set the mood for the whole gathering. Remember, they are taking as big of a step showing up for this study as you are hosting a small group! Don't try to do things exactly like another host; do them in a way that fits you. Admit when you don't have an answer and apologize when you make a mistake. Your group will love you for it and you'll sleep better at night.

3. PREPARE FOR YOUR MEETING AHEAD OF TIME. Review the session and write down your responses to each question. Pay special attention to the PUTTING IT INTO PRACTICE section that focuses on applying what you have learned in each lesson. This section will also help your group live what the Bible teaches, not just talk about it.

4. PRAY FOR YOUR GROUP MEMBERS BY NAME. Before your group arrives, take a few moments and pray for each member by name. You may want to review the Our Prayers & Praise section at least once a week. Ask God to use your time together to touch the heart of each person in your group. Expect God to lead you to whomever he wants you to encourage or challenge in a special way. If you listen, God will surely lead.

5. WHEN YOU ASK A QUESTION, BE PATIENT. Someone will eventually respond. Sometimes people need a moment or two of silence to think about the question. If silence doesn't bother you, it won't bother anyone else. After someone responds, affirm the response with a simple "thanks" or "great answer." Then ask, "How about somebody else?" or "Would someone who hasn't shared like to add anything?" Be sensitive to new people or reluctant members who aren't ready to say, pray, or do anything. If you give them a safe setting, they will blossom over time. If someone in your group is a wallflower who sits silently through every session, consider talking to that person privately and encouraging them to participate. Let them know how important they are to you—that they are loved and appreciated, and that the group would value their input. Remember, still water often runs deep.

6. PROVIDE TRANSITIONS BETWEEN QUESTIONS. Ask if anyone would like to read the paragraph or Bible passage. Don't call on anyone, but ask for a volunteer, and then be patient until someone begins. Be sure to thank the person who reads aloud.

7. BREAK INTO SMALLER GROUPS OCCASIONALLY. With a greater opportunity to talk in a small circle, people will connect more with the study, apply more quickly what they're learning, and ultimately get more out of their small group experience. A small circle also encourages a quiet person to participate and tends to minimize the effects of a more vocal or dominant member.

8. SMALL CIRCLES ARE ALSO HELPFUL DURING PRAYER TIME. People who are unaccustomed to praying aloud will feel more comfortable trying it with just two or three others. Also, prayer requests won't take as much time, so circles will have more time to actually pray. When you gather back with the whole group, you can have one person from each circle briefly update everyone on the prayer requests from their subgroups. The other great aspect of subgrouping is that it fosters leadership development. As you ask people in the group to facilitate discussion or to lead a prayer circle, it gives them a small leadership step that can build their confidence.

9. ROTATE FACILITATORS OCCASIONALLY. You may be perfectly capable of hosting each time, but you will help others grow in their faith and gifts if you give them opportunities to host the group.

10. ONE FINAL CHALLENGE (FOR NEW OR FIRST-TIME HOSTS). Before your first opportunity to lead, look up each of the six passages listed below. Read each one as a devotional exercise to help prepare you with a shepherd's heart. Trust us on this one. If you do this, you will be more than ready for your first meeting.

When he saw the crowds, he had compassion on them, because they were harassed and helpless, like sheep without a shepherd. Then he said to his disciples, "The harvest is plentiful but the workers are few. Ask the Lord of the harvest, therefore to send out workers into his harvest field."
MATTHEW 9:36–38 (NIV)

"I am the good shepherd; I know my sheep and my sheep know me—just as the Father knows me and I know the Father—and I lay down my life for the sheep."
JOHN 10:14–15 (NIV)

Be shepherds of God's flock that is under your care, watching over them—not because you must, but because you are willing, as God wants you to be; not pursuing dishonest gain, but eager to serve; not lording it over those entrusted to you, but being examples to the flock. And when the Chief Shepherd appears, you will receive the crown of glory that will never fade away.
1 PETER 5:2–4 (NIV)

Therefore, if you have any encouragement from being united with Christ, if any comfort from his love, if any common sharing in the Spirit, if any tenderness and compassion, then make my joy complete by being like-minded, having the same love, being one in spirit and of one mind. Do nothing out of selfish ambition or vain conceit. Rather, in humility value others above yourselves, not looking to your own interests but each of you to the interests of the others. In your relationships with one another, have the same mindset as Christ Jesus.
PHILIPPIANS 2:1–5 (NIV)

Let us hold unswervingly to the hope we profess, for he who promised is faithful. And let us consider how we may spur one another on toward love and good deeds, not giving up meeting together, as some are in the habit of doing, but encouraging one another—and all the more as you see the Day approaching.
HEBREWS 10:23–25 (NIV)

But we were gentle among you, like a mother caring for her little children. We loved you so much that we were delighted to share with you not only the gospel of God but our lives as well, because you had become so dear to us . . . For you know that we dealt with each of you as a father deals with his own children, encouraging, comforting and urging you to live lives worthy of God, who calls you into his kingdom and glory.
1 THESSALONIANS 2:7–8, 11–12 (NIV)

FREQUENTLY ASKED QUESTIONS

HOW LONG WILL THIS GROUP MEET?

This study includes seven sessions. We encourage your group to add an extra session for a celebration. In your final session, each group member may decide if he or she desires to continue on for another study. At that time, you may also want to do some informal evaluation, discuss your group guidelines, and decide which study you want to do next. We recommend you visit **PastorRick.com** for more video-based small group studies.

WHO IS THE HOST?

The host is the person who coordinates and facilitates your group meetings. In addition to a host, we encourage you to select one or more group members to lead your group discussions. Several other responsibilities can be rotated, including refreshments, prayer requests, worship, or keeping up with those who miss a meeting. Shared ownership in the group helps everybody grow.

WHERE DO WE FIND NEW GROUP MEMBERS?

Recruiting new members can be a challenge for groups, especially new groups with just a few people, or existing groups that lose a few people along the way. We encourage you to use the Circles of Life diagram on page 203 of this study guide to brainstorm a list of people from your workplace, church, school, neighborhood, family, and so on. Then pray for the people on each member's list. Allow each member to invite several people from their list. Some groups fear that newcomers will interrupt the intimacy that members have built over time. However, groups that welcome newcomers generally gain strength with the infusion of "new blood." Remember, the next person you add just might become a friend for eternity. Logistically, groups find different ways to add members. Some groups remain permanently open, while others choose to open periodically, such as at the beginning or end of a study. If your group becomes too large for easy, face-to-face conversations, you can subgroup, forming a second discussion group in another room.

HOW DO WE HANDLE THE CHILDCARE NEEDS IN OUR GROUP?

Childcare needs must be handled very carefully. This is a sensitive issue. We suggest you seek creative solutions as a group. One common solution is to have the adults meet in the living room and share the cost of a babysitter (or two) who can be with the kids in another part of the house. Another popular option is to have one supervised home for the kids and a second home (close by) for the adults. If desired, the adults could rotate the responsibility of providing a lesson for the kids. This last option is great with school-age kids and can be a huge blessing to families.

CIRCLES OF LIFE

Discover Who You Can Connect In Community

Use this chart to help carry out one of the values in the Group Guidelines on page 202, to "Welcome Newcomers."

Follow this simple three-step process:

1. List one to two people in each circle.

2. Prayerfully select one person or couple from your list and tell your group about them.

3. Give them a call and invite them to your next meeting. Over fifty percent of those invited to a small group say, "Yes!"

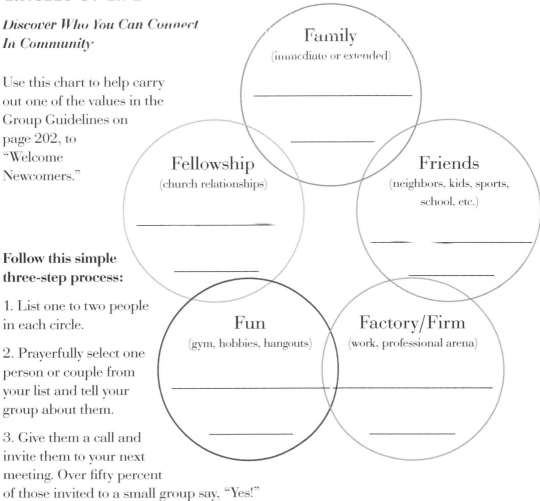

Family
(immediate or extended)

Fellowship
(church relationships)

Friends
(neighbors, kids, sports, school, etc.)

Fun
(gym, hobbies, hangouts)

Factory/Firm
(work, professional arena)

SMALL GROUP GUIDELINES

It's a good idea for every group to put words to their shared values, expectations, and commitments. Such guidelines will help you avoid unspoken agendas and unmet expectations. We recommend you discuss your guidelines during Session One in order to lay the foundation for a healthy group experience. Feel free to modify anything that does not work for your group.

WE AGREE TO THE FOLLOWING VALUES:

CLEAR PURPOSE
To grow healthy spiritual lives by building a healthy small group community.

GROUP ATTENDANCE
To give priority to the group meeting (call if I am absent or late).

SAFE ENVIRONMENT
To create a safe place where people can be heard and feel loved (no quick answers, snap judgments, or simple fixes).

BE CONFIDENTIAL
To keep anything that is shared strictly confidential and within the group.

CONFLICT RESOLUTION
To avoid gossip and to immediately resolve any concerns by following the principles of Matthew 18:15–17.

SPIRITUAL HEALTH
To give group members permission to speak into my life and help me live a healthy, balanced spiritual life that is pleasing to God.

LIMIT OUR FREEDOM
To limit our freedom by not serving or consuming alcohol during small group meetings or events so as to avoid causing a another brother or sister to stumble (1 Corinthians 8:1–13; Romans 14:19–21).

WELCOME NEWCOMERS
To invite friends who might benefit from this study, and warmly welcome newcommers.

BUILD RELATIONSHIPS
To get to know the other members of the group and pray for them regularly.

OTHER _____

We have also discussed and agree on the following items:

CHILDCARE _____

STARTING TIME _____

ENDING TIME _____

If you haven't already done so, take a few minutes to fill out the
SMALL GROUP CALENDAR on page 206.

OUR PRAYERS & PRAISE

This is a place where you can write each other's requests for prayer. You can also make a note when God answers a prayer. Pray for each other's requests. If you're new to group prayer, it's okay to pray silently or to pray by using just one sentence:

"God, please help _____ _____ to _____."

DATE/PERSON	PRAYER REQUEST	PRAISE REPORT

DATE/PERSON	PRAYER REQUEST	PRAISE REPORT

SMALL GROUP CALENDAR

Healthy groups share responsibilities and group ownership. It might take some time for this to develop. Shared ownership ensures that responsibility for the group doesn't fall to one person. Use the calendar to keep track of social events, mission projects, birthdays, or days off. Complete this calendar at your first or second meeting. Planning ahead will increase attendance and shared ownership.

DATE	SESSION	LOCATION	FACILITATOR	SNACK OR MEAL
	ONE			
	TWO			
	THREE			
	FOUR			
	FIVE			
	SIX			
	BONUS			
	CELEBRATION			

SMALL GROUP ROSTER

NAME	PHONE	EMAIL

Answer Key

SESSION ONE: THE PURPOSE OF PRAYER

- Prayer is an act of DEDICATION.

- Prayer is an act of COMMUNICATION.

- Prayer is an act of SUPPLICATION.

- Prayer is an act of COOPERATION.

SESSION TWO: HOW TO PRAY WITH CONFIDENCE

- God is a CARING Father.

- God is a CONSISTENT Father.

- God is a CLOSE Father.

  ○ God is never TOO BUSY FOR ME.

  ○ God loves to MEET MY NEEDS.

  ○ God is SYMPATHETIC TO MY HURTS.

- God is a COMPETENT Father.

SESSION THREE: THE PATTERN FOR PRAYER (PART 1)

- I remember HOW MUCH GOD LOVES ME.

- I tell God HOW MUCH I LOVE HIM.

- I offer my life TO BE USED FOR GOD'S PURPOSES.

- I give God MY PAIN AND SORROW.

- I trust GOD TO MEET ALL MY NEEDS.

SESSION FOUR: THE PATTERN FOR PRAYER (PART 2)

- I admit MY FAULTS.

- I release THOSE WHO HAVE HURT ME.

- I ask God TO GUARD MY HEART.

- I depend ON GOD'S POWER.

- I praise God FOR ULTIMATE VICTORY.

SESSION FIVE: PRAYING FOR A BREAKTHROUGH

- Let God SPEAK TO ME BEFORE I SPEAK TO HIM.

- Focus MY ATTENTION ON GOD.

- Express MY DESIRES WITH EMOTION.

- Demonstrate MY SERIOUSNESS.

- Thank God FOR HIS LOVE AND PROMISES.

- Humbly CONFESS MY SIN.

SESSION SIX: HOW TO PRAY IN A CRISIS

- Turn TO GOD FOR HELP.

  ○ Remember HOW BIG GOD IS.

  ○ Remember WHAT GOD HAS DONE.

  ○ Remember WHAT GOD HAS PROMISED.

  ○ Appeal TO GOD'S CHARACTER.

- Admit MY INADEQUACY.

- Rely ON GOD'S RESOURCES.

- Relax IN FAITH.

- Thank God IN ADVANCE.

- Expect God TO TURN BATTLES INTO BLESSINGS.

BONUS SESSION: WHY DOESN'T GOD ALWAYS ANSWER THE FIRST TIME I PRAY?

- Praying persistently KEEPS ME FOCUSED ON GOD.

- Praying persistently TEACHES ME ABOUT MYSELF.

  ○ God will TEST me before he BLESSES me.

- Praying persistently TESTS MY PRIORITIES.

- Praying persistently TESTS MY MATURITY.

  ○ PATIENCE is a mark of maturity.

- Praying persistently TESTS MY FAITH.

  ○ When MY REQUEST IS NOT RIGHT, God says NO.

  ○ When I AM NOT RIGHT, God says GROW.

  ○ When THE TIMING IS NOT RIGHT, God says SLOW.

  ○ When MY REQUEST AND MY CHARACTER AND THE TIMING are all lined up, God says, GO.

NOTES

NOTES

NOTES

NOTES

NOTES

NOTES

NOTES

NOTES

PRAYER PAGES

PRAYERS

PRAYERS

PRAYERS

PRAYERS

PRAYERS

PRAYERS

PRAYERS

PRAYERS

PRAYERS

PRAYERS

PRAYERS

PRAYERS

PRAYERS

_____

_____

_____

_____

_____

_____

_____

_____

_____

_____

_____

_____

_____

_____

_____

_____

_____

PRAYERS

PRAYERS

PRAYERS

PRAYERS

PRAYERS

PRAYERS

_____

_____

_____

_____

_____

_____

_____

_____

_____

_____

_____

_____

_____

_____

_____

_____

_____

_____

PHOTOGRAPERS

Aaron Burden/unsplash

Alfred Leung/unsplash

Amy Humphries/unsplash

Andreas Selter

Austin Neill/unsplash

Braxton Stuntz

Brian Uyeda

Buddy Owens

Clarisse Meyer/unsplash

Dairui Chen/unsplash

Dan Gold/unsplash

Dawn Severdia

Dave S Wallace/iStockphoto

Diana Fell/unsplash

Doug Berry/iStockphoto

Elizabeth Lies/unsplash

Enrapture Media/unsplash

Ferdinand Stohr/unsplash

Frank Mckenna/unsplash

Georg Wolf/unsplash

haveseen/istock

Hxdbzxy/iStockphoto

Ishan Seefromthesky

Jeremy Elder

Joe Rosh/iStockphoto

Kanonsky/iStockphoto

Jakob Owens/unsplash

Jan Erik Waider/unsplash

Jeremy Bishop/unsplash

John Konrad/unsplash

Jorge Gordo/unsplash

Joshua Fuller/unsplash

Marianne Heino/unsplash

Matt Briney/unsplash

Matthew Kane/unsplash

Milada Vigerova/unsplash

Monty Lov/unsplash

O.C. Gonzalez/unsplash

OneInchPunch/iStockphoto

Pedro Lastra/unsplash

Rebecca Dawson Thacher

Rob Bye/unsplash

Ron Thomas/iStockphoto

Ryan Loughlin/unsplash

Sam Soffes/unsplash

Smitt/iStockphoto

Stuart Guest Smith/unsplash

Tim Mossholder/unsplash

Toltek/iStockphoto

Trace Rouda/iStockphoto

Velvetfish/iStockphoto

Vladimir Kudinov/unsplash

Westboundary Photography

Zeny Rosalina/unsplash

Zeus Z/unsplash

40 DAYS OF PRAYER
Small Group Study Guide
Edition 1.0
Copyright © 2017 Rick Warren

30021 Comercio, Rancho Santa Margarita, CA 92688

ISBN: 978-1-4228-0464-3

Printed in the U.S.A.